A GIFT FROM
ADVERSITY

A GIFT FROM
ADVERSITY

**OVERCOMING SEXUAL ABUSE, DOMESTIC
VIOLENCE, BULLYING, AND HOMELESSNESS**

JURI LOVE

 **BOOK**LOGIX˙
Alpharetta, GA

The author has tried to recreate events, locations, and conversations from her memories of them. The author has made every effort to give credit to the source of any images, quotes, or other material contained within and obtain permissions when feasible.

ISBN: 978-1-61005-970-1 – Paperback
eISBN: 978-1-61005-971-8 – ePub
eISBN: 978-1-61005-972-5 – mobi

Library of Congress Control Number: 2020916480

Printed in the United States of America   0 8 2 8 2 0

♾This paper meets the requirements of ANSI/NISO Z39.48-1992 (Permanence of Paper)

Cover photo by Taiga Kunii
Cover design by Rebecacovers

The sooner you can find the courage to accept your adversity, the sooner you can pave a positive path in your precious life.

CONTENTS

Like a perfect blue sky influences the color of the ocean

Your bright smile becomes someone's smile

Like a raging storm can destroy everything

Your agony can destroy somebody

If you think you just hit rock bottom

There must be a meaning

You don't have to force yourself to move out of it

One way is to be still and observe

"Hope" may be created from there

"A Gift from Adversity"

A gift is YOU who decided to read my story

A gift is this splendor and beauty of sharing this very moment with you

Everything will be okay even if you are going through adversity

Because you are breathing now

Because you are smiling now

Because you are crying now

And because you are helping me now by reading my story

Even if you are going through the hardest time in your life

You will be okay

Because you are alive now

CAUTION

This is my life story. My soul is laid bare in the pages that follow and my writing depicts my perspective. Please know some of this material is disturbing. I don't mean to offend anyone. Please accept my apology in advance if I do offend you as you read my story. I can't thank you enough for expending your time to learn about my life experience.

The Dead Sea

IN THE SUMMER OF 2009, I WAS AT THE DEAD SEA IN Israel. Recently separated from my ex-husband (first husband) and living out of a small rented room, I chatted with a fun gay friend from Israel whom I met in Spain and told him I was depressed. He asked me to come to visit him in Israel, so there I was.

I noticed many young soldiers armed with long rifles on the bus as I traveled to the Dead Sea from Jerusalem. Out of the window on my right, the ocher-colored mountains stood proudly. On my left was the Dead Sea, adorned by a dim mountain skyline on the Jordan side.

During the intense ten-day trip, I met one lost soul from America in Eilat, located at the southern tip of Israel, sharing the border of Egypt and Jordan near the Red Sea. A few days after we met, we decided to meet again at the Dead Sea, where we swam in our regular clothes without bothering to changing into swimsuits. We floated in the warm water, viewing the mystical Israeli night sky together. Both of us were crying for different reasons, but as our tears dissolved in the warm salt lake, neither of us noticed how many tears melted in the Dead Sea. Such a mysterious salt lake, the surface situated 430.5 meters (1,421 ft) below sea level. It seemed ironic to be there, both of us struggling at the worst point in our lives, hitting rock bottom at the lowest point of the earth. We were both emotionally exhausted: about life, hope, achievement, and failure. We felt lost and astray.

While floating in the Dead Sea, my new friend shared a verse from the wise poet Rumi:

> *When water gets caught in habitual whirlpools,*
> *dig a way out through the bottom to the ocean.*
>
> *There is a secret medicine given only to*
> *those who hurt so hard they can't hope.*

It seemed so fitting to be at the lowest point on earth, letting go of our bodies and broken souls, afloat on the dark Dead Sea. We stared at the blurred stars from evaporated saltwater, wishful but without hope, yet finding solace and comfort as we contemplated Rumi's verse.

Here is what I interpreted from this wisdom-filled passage: If you are looking for the way to the top when you are truly down and at rock bottom, instead of struggling and fighting your way up, simply float, like a body on the Dead Sea, held buoyant by your tears and fears. You don't need special strength or courage. If you are falling, let yourself fall to the deepest level. It is there that you will rise and heal. Now I can understand that Rumi was right.

CHAPTER 1

Heroes Among Us

NOVEMBER 15, 2013. I WAS THE FOCUS OF A BRIGHT spotlight beaming from somewhere above. I was introduced to center court during an NBA Boston Celtics game at the TD Garden in Boston, Massachusetts. After a short video depicting the work and accomplishments of Genuine Voices, the organization I founded and in which I served as president, my name was called, echoing through the loudspeakers. Seventeen thousand people seemed to rise in unison, filling the Garden from the floor to the rafters. As people cheered and found their feet, I felt as if I were standing at ground zero during a roaring tsunami. The Garden walls shook and the crowd's applause erupted like thunder, surrounding me from 360 degrees. My hand shook as it struggled to grasp a large trophy—presented by the Boston Celtics and sponsored by the Massachusetts State Lottery, the Sports Hub 98.5 FM, and Comcast SportsNet—while I waved frantically to thank the gracious crowd with the other.

The award I received was called Heroes Among Us. A beautiful diamond-shaped glass trophy had my name engraved on it and a message that stated, "Heroes Among Us: The Boston Celtics salute your exemplary efforts and invaluable contribution to our community." During the Celtics game versus the Portland Trail Blazers, the announcer's voice said from the jumbo speakers: "Juri Love, a musician since the age of three, understands the importance of music in young people's lives. A proud promoter of the arts, Juri is the president and founder of Genuine Voices, a nonprofit that teaches music to juvenile offenders and at-risk kids in the Greater Boston Area. Through music, Genuine Voices strives to build their creativity and increase their resilience. To date, thanks to Juri's leadership, more than six hundred at-risk youths are being provided music lessons!"

It all felt like a dream. In addition to the award, I was given four tickets to the game—and premium tickets at that. Our seats were located directly behind the CEO of the Celtics, second row, courtside. A driver was sent to chauffeur us to the Garden, where we were escorted by the friendly staff to a private entrance only accessible by authorized people. I had never experienced such excitement or a sense of pride in my life. If receiving an award and accolades by way of an ovation from seventeen thousand fans wasn't enough, during half-time I was approached by a gentleman who introduced himself as Steve. "Congratulations, my name is Steve," he began with a solid, warm handshake. "I am the owner of the team!" I felt so privileged and honored. It was Mr. Steve Pagliuca who had come to congratulate me.

The night was incredible and unforgettable. Under the brightest and warmest spotlight at the center court of the TD Garden, I received pure cheers, adoration, and appreciation in support of my work. To describe what it was like, it felt as if I was in the center of huge energy that could bend the air. I will never forget that moment.

When I came to Boston in 1998, I knew no one, not a single person I could call a friend. But here I was, fifteen years later, with thousands of people recognizing me, acknowledging my work, and sending me their gracious love and positive energy. I accepted this as a reward for working through many of the struggles in my life. I knew there would be more difficulties to contend with, but at this moment, I was humbled, yet very proud of myself, my work, and my perseverance to overcome all the adversity laid before me. To receive this reward, and an award from the Boston Celtics, meant the world to me. Thank you for choosing me to be one of your recipients.

I received this award because I was the founder and president of the not-for-profit organization Genuine Voices. I started the organization when I was twenty-six years old and functioned as its president for twelve years. Through Genuine Voices, we taught music, especially hip-hop and production, in juvenile detention centers and certain after-school programs. Because of our mission and our work, many kids became inspired through music and some even changed the course of their lives. Once students focused on creating music, amazing things happened. They built self-esteem and pride, and in doing so, the resilience to overcome many of the obstacles they faced. In some cases, music replaced drugs and violence, and for many kept them off the streets and out of trouble.

Genuine Voices afforded me an amazing opportunity to work with juvenile offenders and "high-risk" youth for twelve years of my life. Most of these young people were broken, portraying toughness because of significant amounts of trauma that never appropriately healed. They all required positive influences in their lives when there were simply not many good role models around them. The majority came from dysfunctional families. Many of the kids I met had parents serving jail time or were dealing or hooked on drugs. Many lived or spent time with foster families, were abused, or witnessed gun violence at a very young age.

Can we expect a five-year-old child who witnessed his father get shot and die in front of his own eyes to be completely normal without rebelling or acting out in some way when he becomes a teenager? When his father is killed by gun violence and his mother is addicted to drugs, a child becomes custody of the State. This typically results in a child being raised by foster parents. Most foster homes try their best to give that child a secure environment to grow in. With limited resources, however, and usually other children in that home in need of attention, is it really surprising that many of these damaged children find their way to a troubled path?

I had a student who participated and performed his original rap at one of our fundraisers after his release. He had been in and out of detention programs since the age of thirteen, mostly on drug-related charges, since he had no idea what another world would look like. Everyone around him was doing the same. His father was in jail, his mother was a heavy drug user, even his uncles were into drugs. His grandmother raised him.

After he turned eighteen, I brought him to Rockport, Massachusetts, for sea kayaking with some of the volunteer teachers from Genuine Voices who taught music to him. When there, he informed me it was the first time he had ever seen an ocean. He thanked me from his heart after having a blast navigating the shoreline of the Atlantic Ocean in a kayak. Tears flowed from my heart, trying to imagine the eighteen years he had lived, so young, so alone, with no one who believed in him.

After twelve years behind and in front of the scenes at Genuine Voices, I decided it was time to close in 2014. I was spent, tired of the constant struggle dealing with the system and the constant fundraising. I was also struggling in my personal life, having had two miscarriages around the same time. It was an unimaginably difficult decision, but I knew it was time. I had tried my best, learned a tremendous amount of life lessons, and met so many beautiful people who became lifelong friends. But in the end, I decided to let go of my vision and venture because of what I like to call "enough universal signs."

CHAPTER 2

Process

I WAS BORN IN A SMALL TOWN IN JAPAN WHERE ONLY four thousand people lived. It was located in the very rural countryside, at the base of majestic mountains including Mt. Fuji, the highest mountain in Japan, and surrounded by nature. Everyone knew everyone, in a good and bad way. It was nice that all your neighbors were known acquaintances, but not so pleasant in that all your neighbors knew your business. I was a happy and energetic girl who was always playing outside, exploring the small world in which I was raised. I loved playing in the woods and streams, not so much climbing trees, but hiking and being creative. My family had a small farm where they grew lots of different vegetables. I was good at helping in the garden, weeding, planting, and harvesting. I loved digging giant potatoes, plucking fresh tomatoes, eggplants, and green beans, and searching out hidden cucumbers—and eating them all fresh!

My mother owned a rock café and played music in a rock band. She was unique, not a quiet, typical Japanese woman. She was outgoing, funny, fashionable, and passionate, giving birth to me when she was twenty-three. Mom was a hard worker, always busy, so I was mostly surrounded by my father, three uncles, grandparents, and little sister growing up.

My mother brought me into her rock band at the tender age of four. She played the drums and I dabbled on the keyboards. I remember practicing with the band until late into the night. I learned all the songs by memory because I was just learning to read music and wasn't familiar with chord charts. I played everything by ear, using the sound of the music to guide me when I couldn't recall a chord. Mom was very proud of me. I remember playing my first gig not long after I joined the band. Before the concert, my mom, who was handy with a needle and thread, altered her wedding dress so I'd have something dressy to perform in. After seeing me in the frilly gown, however, she realized a white fluffy dress was not "rock 'n' roll" enough for the stage, so she added an orange scarf to the outfit, draping it around my waist. I may have been a young child, but I was a strong-willed, opinionated young woman, a trait I still possess to this day. "This is such a mismatch!" I cried. "Orange and white don't go well. I don't want to wear this around my waist."

Nonetheless, she forced me to wear it, leading to a meltdown. None of my tears, fussing, or ranting about how embarrassed I was would change her mind. Despite my tender age of four, I was a strong soul who fought for what I believed. My tears exploded into a full tantrum, but sadly all that resulted was my not playing the gig. I remember crying backstage and listening to the performance, thinking how much better the band would have sounded if I were on stage with them, contributing to the sound.

Even so, being surrounded by music continued to inspire me and I practiced incessantly. Years later, when I was twenty-one years old, I did perform with my mom on vocal and my stepdad on bass guitar, on stage together. Still in the role of fashion police, she insisted that I wear a tall, floppy red hat on my head, which of course I felt was a mismatch to my long yellow dress. This time, however, I didn't throw a tantrum because I knew I'd be leaving for America soon after the concert. So, I made the best of it to make my mother happy, and we amicably performed as a family. The song we rendered was the same tune we had rehearsed all those years back when I was supposed to perform with my mother's band at age four.

When I was growing up, my mom was always busy working at the rock café she owned. I rarely saw her, except for band practice. I missed her a lot. As a means to stay close and connected, she suggested we exchange journals. I would document all that happened during the day and leave it for her to read when she came home, late after I went to bed. She, in turn, would share her day and respond to items I had written. I truly enjoyed this exchange and looked forward to new entries every day. I also loved playing the piano and taking private piano lessons. I also took an abacus class when attending elementary school. Generally speaking, I was a pretty happy girl in my early childhood.

One very cold night in January 1983, my mom did not return home. We looked everywhere and my dad was beside himself with worry. Given the cold, we were quite concerned for her well-being. My dad told my grandparents and they, too, started to look for her. I recall being so scared for her and spent most of the night crying on my futon, hoping desperately that nothing terrible had happened to my mother.

The next morning my maternal grandmother called my father saying my mom would not be coming home. I didn't comprehend what had happened, nor could I conceive any inkling of the hell this would initiate. Had I had any idea how this event would impact the rest of my childhood and the rest of my life, I might have reacted differently. But I was only seven years old. What could I have possibly done differently?

Since that day, I wished incessantly my mom would return and life could resume as it was. Exchanging our journals, going to band practice together, and other little things, like strawberry picking, were some of my simple wishes—wishes that never came to fruition.

PLAYING DEAD

I was eight when my parents divorced.

One day my mom, her mother, and a lady I had never met visited our house. We all sat at a little table called a kotatsu. The table consisted of a green comforter covering its wood top and a little electric heater inside. Everyone was sitting on a tatami mat around the kotatsu. Even today, I can still picture it in my mind, the pattern of the green print that I stared at the whole time the adults were talking about various difficult issues. Now, I understand who that unknown woman was, but at the age of eight, how could I ever guess that the professionally dressed woman was a divorce lawyer? My dad, paternal grandparents, mom, maternal grandmother (my maternal grandfather was killed in a car accident a year before I was born), and the attorney were talking intensely.

It seemed everyone was avoiding eye contact, except for the divorce attorney. She was sitting next to me; I was frustrated because I wanted to sit next to my mom. I had not seen her for about a year at that point. Everyone was crying. I don't remember any of their conversations, but vividly recall the green overlap covering of the kotatsu, which was my focus. I stared at it intently, fighting the rising fear emanating deep from my heart.

All of a sudden my tears started to flow uncontrollably. I'm not sure what triggered this outburst in emotion since I did not understand what was going on. I think it stemmed from the fact that I could not sit next to my mom. I missed her so much, and to see her in tears, eyes averted, looking down . . . it was overwhelming. I became angry when this unknown lady, a stranger to me, pulled out a white handkerchief and began to wipe my tears. I fought the urge to slap her hand and tell her to stop, but of course, I could not. She kept wiping my tears, trying to soothe me, but I was inconsolable and just hated her and that white handkerchief all the more.

It was then, at the tender age of eight, that I experienced hate for the first time. I knew the word but had never really understood the feeling, the unbridled agony and burning malice that erupts deep within your gut. It was so strong and it consumed me; I could taste it. I hated it all—that day, that lady, and most of all, the despair that seemed to permeate our home. To this day, whenever I see a white handkerchief, anger flutters within me. It triggers a connection in my mind with the divorce lawyer's handkerchief and reminds me of that sad day.

Given all I have come to know over the years, I believe my mom and grandmother did the right thing in filing for divorce. When I was old enough to understand, I realized how my mom was being abused. She explained that she had tried to take me and my sister, but my father and grandfather came to her mother's house and snatched us back. This I don't recall. Many years later in 2003, after my maternal grandmother was diagnosed with cancer, and when I visited her from America, she told me the story. My mother had truly tried to gain custody of my sister and me, but my dad wouldn't let her, which resulted in the hiring of an attorney and that painful day.

I still cannot understand why my mom would be denied custody of her children when she was being abused. Perhaps due to Japanese customs, spousal abuse is more tolerated, such that it isn't reported except in severe cases. I do recall one incident when I was very young, probably about four. I went to my parents' room on the second floor to show them a drawing I made. The shoji sliding door was closed, but I heard my mom crying, my dad yelling at her, and other muffled noises, and I saw her being beaten up against the shoji wall. I recall being scared and so frustrated that I didn't know what to do. I still regret not opening that door and doing something to help her, but I had no idea what to do. I still remember that fear vividly.

After my parents' divorce, my life changed forever. While at the time I knew my mom was leaving my father, she didn't explain why until much later in my life. I was young but mature for my age, having seen a lot of life early on.

I was doing well in school, getting good grades and excelling in scholastic sports, both on the track and volleyball teams. Yet despite outward appearances and beneath the visible outgoing persona, there was the inner me erecting a wall between people and my heart. I wanted no one to see my weakness; for that matter, I wanted no one to know my mother had left (which was impossible in a small, rural town). I hated people trying to comfort me or providing unnecessary compassion; I thought it patronizing and annoying. I wanted to block my mother's leaving and simply be left alone to live my life. I recall vividly my father's coworker giving me an unexpected small gift such as underwear because I didn't have a mother. I wanted to throw it away. I didn't want anyone's pity or to be thought of differently because my mom left. Gifts and kindness, no matter how well-intended, didn't bandage what I felt or change a larger problem, which no one suspected or knew.

My father was a violent man. Sadly, my clearest memories of him were beating my mom and my uncle, whom I believed suffered from alcoholism and mental health issues. It seemed there was always violence in the house. My grandpa never hit me, but he often physically and verbally abused my mentally challenged uncle. After Mom left, my father's frustration and violence shifted toward me. He began to physically, mentally, and even sexually abuse me. The violence escalated until, at age thirteen, I felt the only way for me to survive was to escape the man I called a perpetrator—not a father. He was a sick criminal who was never caught for justice and never will be. It will mean nothing to me if he gets arrested for what he has done to me at this point in my life since it was so long ago and I would rather focus on what I have than what I lost.

My abuse wasn't limited to the home. One day, the kids at school were bullying me for not having a colorful lunch. They made fun of my lunch, saying it was all brown, void of color, or anything "good." I returned home that day, hurt from this unprovoked harassment, and asked my paternal grandmother if she might include some colorful items in my lunch to preclude this pestering. She informed me curtly, "You are not my priority; your father is my priority. Your mother left you and I am being nice enough to make your lunch. Since you don't appreciate it, starting today, you must make your lunch." She continued as if I were baggage left by my mother. "It is not my place to raise you, and I don't wish to, but your mother left, so I am forced to do so without a choice."

My grandmother was not a loving person. This may be why my father became the monster he was, spawned through hate and abuse, but I might be completely wrong. She redirected her loathing for my mother at me, blaming my every mistake on my mom's

15

parenting. A typical insult might be, "Your mother, who left you, must have taught you that way . . . explains why you are so stupid."

Between the bullying at school and a dismal home situation, this once-happy child found life anything but appealing. Being a young teenager is difficult enough without the pressures of bullying and abuse weighing in. I knew I couldn't live this way and turned inward to figure out a solution. I decided to tell my father about what happened, hoping he might speak to my grandmother and perhaps help with the bullying at school as well.

It was naïve on my part and a big mistake to expect a rational response from my father. Instead, he dragged me to the kitchen, began yelling and cursing at me, grabbed me by the hair, and pounded my head on the dining table several times. He threw me against the sliding glass door and kicked me in the stomach so hard I could not breathe or make any sound. My grandpa tried to help calm my father down from the other side of the door but to no avail. Whether my grandfather was afraid my father's temper would turn on him, I don't know for sure, but what I am sure of is the door never opened and no one came to rescue me. My father informed my grandpa that how he dealt with me was none of his (my grandfather's) business.

Through all the pain—the dizziness in my head from contact with the table, the throbbing in my stomach and ribs from the violent kicks, and the laboring in my lungs—I could focus on only one thing: how to escape. Not just from that moment, but from the madness that had become my life.

Even today, in my forties, I can still hear my hyperventilating, the wheezing sound inside me as I struggled to catch my next breath. The picture remains vividly etched in my mind of being thrown against the sliding glass door, desperately hoping it wouldn't shatter and slice up my body. When my father left for the bathroom, I summoned my courage, laced my running shoes, and, as silently as possible, raced away. The dark, dead night held more promise than remaining at home.

I ran as fast as I could to my best friend's house. I don't recall what time it was, but I remember it was dark. I had no idea what kind of car my father was driving, but I knew the sound of the engine. When I was running, I heard the familiar sound of my father's car, and it shook me to the core. If he was mad before, he'd be furious that I'd run off. I hid along the roadside, running out of sight from the car. My father knew my best friend and figured that was where I'd run to, so I arrived to see his car parked in front of my friend's house, which completely froze me and my heart. Instead of losing hope, I went to another friend's house nearby. My friend and her family were shocked to see me so late at night. Nonetheless, they were kind enough to shelter me. We called my friend whose house my dad was at, and she told me my father entered her house and began searching for me, despite being told I was not there.

However, he somehow found where I was and entered aggressively. My friend's parents asked him to calm down. I did not dare look into my father's eyes; they seemed demonic, as though he was possessed. He tried to punch me from across the table. Fortunately, my friend's father grabbed him and I was able to dodge another painful punch. In the end, though, I returned home with him. The physical abuse continued, but for some reason, I still thought he loved me and I harbored a hope that the violence would cease. Sadly, I was wrong.

Once home, things only escalated. It was bad enough that I was an object of scorn. That I suffered physical mistreatment and verbal abuse, constantly being ridiculed as "stupid," a "whore," "only causing trouble." But when I thought it couldn't get worse,

"IT" started. Not only was my youth crushed by divorce and physical and emotional abuse, but now my innocence would be stolen. It was difficult to maintain faith in anything, and my hope for the future all but vanished.

One time, my father forced me to take a bath with him. I refused; I didn't want to take my clothes off, but he forced me to get undressed. Once we were both naked before taking a bath, he grabbed my skinny hand and forced me to touch his testicles. He said they were "very soft and nice." I could not look at his eyes, but I could hear the weird sounds he made, sounds I would never want to replay in my head. Sadly, even now, that moment and sound sometimes return to me outside of my control. I felt like I died being forced to do this. I was embarrassed, ashamed, and wanted to even kill myself. Unfortunately, the worst day of my life was yet to come. Even today, that feeling of melancholy, as if the sky is falling, still finds me when I think of it.

One night (I don't recall the date and time), when I was still thirteen, I was sleeping soundly next to him (in Japan, due to space issues, we often share a futon with family members), and I awoke to a strange sensation in my private area. As this happened, I felt his hot breath and kisses upon my neck. His warm breath began to find its way around my body. His breathing became faster, his touch more probing and aggressive, touching my breasts and all over the body. The sound, the touch, and the warmth that no one on this earth should ever experience, especially by their biological father.

Then he got out of bed, stood, and started to remove his pants. I knew I had to do something to prevent what was coming, so I made an excuse that I had to go to the bathroom. Instead, I went down to my paternal grandmother's room and crawled into her futon. Knowing my father would erupt into a tantrum, possibly becoming violent, I didn't want to upset him, so I never mentioned what he did and pretended nothing happened.

My grandma asked me why I was in her room and I said I just wanted to be with her. Then my father came in and asked my grandmother to send me upstairs to sleep in his bed. I lay there pretending I was sound asleep and shut my eyes as tight as possible, although I was wide awake and alert.

Ever since I have become sensitive to the littlest of noises and am a very light sleeper. Because of this trauma, I have suffered many years of insomnia and am subject to waking in the night screaming. In my adulthood years, I have tried to especially avoid sleeping around 1 a.m. to 3 a.m. and remain active and alert during that period of the night.

I never want anyone, especially a child, to suffer what I went through. Even today, as I am writing about this incident, I find myself shaking uncontrollably. Tears I thought had dried up after almost three decades of shedding now flow like rain. To still cry after so long gives you some indication of the deepness of this pain. I will undoubtedly bear this anguish for the rest of my life.

Of course, when this happened, so many years back, I had no idea about the magnitude of this incident, and how it would impact the rest of my life. I was a young thirteen-year-old trying to survive in a rural town in Japan.

Sadly, the home wasn't the only place where my life was difficult. I remember bullying at school intensified around the same time as the sexual abuse began. Looking back now, I understand it was pretty serious, but nothing compared to what was happening at home. As a result of the sexual abuse, I think I went into shock and could not speak for about a week. I recall being surrounded by a group of girls at school, making fun of me because I would not talk or respond to their tormenting. They called me crazy, saying I had gone deaf. To some degree, they were correct; I had shut out the world, muting everything to survive another day. My head was numb and my heart had completely frozen.

Years later, my counselor explained this as "playing dead," a reflex to a traumatic event. It is what several animals do, and some humans as well. I was effectively "playing dead" and numbing myself to prevent getting hurt again. It was a defense mechanism and I applied it every day. Of course, I had no way of knowing this means of self-preservation would control the majority of my life. It would rob me of happiness, leaving me to know I deserved to feel it but was unable to do so.

OTHER INCIDENTS

Looking back now, I can see the dysfunction in my house growing up beyond that of my father. I had two unmarried uncles who lived with us. They played a lot of tickling-type games, but often they found their way to my futon and tickled me inappropriately, especially around my private area. I was young, and at the time I thought it was just an extension of play, but I realize now it was completely improper. I do remember it being awkward, but since my uncles were smiling and giggling, it seemed a normal thing. Perhaps I should have read into their laughs, but these were people I loved and trusted, so I went along. Sadly, now I remember that experience as another low point in my life.

I recall one instance when I was four or five years old, and my father was teaching me some English words. I went to my neighbor friend's house, and suddenly, without provocation, her grandfather began kicking me, saying, "You can't even spell in Japanese, you should not speak English." He struck me pretty hard. I have no idea why. Whatever the reason, it instilled a new fear, and I became afraid to learn something new.

I also remember receiving a report card from school. It reflected good grades. My school used a 1–5 system, 5 being the highest, so when I got 4 in one subject my father began to hit me for the mark that didn't measure up to his expectations.

Another time, I traveled with my father for a work trip, which took us near the ocean in a different prefecture. It was fun until one night when his coworkers were drinking, swapping stories, and generally just hanging out in a large, open room. As I happened to pass by, one of my father's coworkers groped my butt. I must have been nine or ten years old. I turned and gave the man a dirty look. I thought my father, who witnessed the action, would defend me and say something, but instead, he laughed with the group, commenting on how embarrassed I looked, which was funny to them. I still remember all too well that feeling of humiliation, and probably will never forget it.

My family greatly enjoyed going to Pachinko, a gambling venue. One of the attractions featured these metal balls you could purchase and spin to fall in slots. If the ball found the correct slot, you could win rewards. My family spent the majority of their free time there because it was within walking distance from my home. I sometimes tagged along or just visited when I had nothing better to do. It was a smoky environment, but at the time no one realized how serious even secondhand smoke was for the lungs and general health, never mind that of a youngster.

I remember picking up the little metal balls that would fall on the floor. I would collect a handful and give them to my father, my grandmother, or my uncles. It was one of the few things they appreciated me doing, and I loved collecting these free balls from the floor just to see their smiles.

Despite the physical, emotional, verbal, and sexual abuse that was going on at home, and the bullying at school, I surprisingly did well in the classroom. I kept taking piano and abacus lessons. I ran track when I was in junior high and played on the volleyball team. I enjoyed the motion of the sports and found release in practicing piano. That was because when I was practicing or participating in sports, my father and other family members didn't bother me. By focusing on school, I not only excelled in my studies, but I escaped the harsh reality of my home life as much as possible.

On one occasion my teacher asked me to compose a song in music class, and I did so well, he invited me to a regional composition competition. I was about eleven, and my composed music piece won a prefecture-level award. I also displayed talent at painting, and one of my artworks was displayed at one of the finer museums in our prefecture. In sixth grade, I also participated in a prefecture-level competition with my abacus and won third place. In track I was fast, running eight hundred meters with the best time in seventh grade, which was 2:53.

All these extracurricular activities allowed me to pretend nothing was amiss at home. In short, it allowed me to hide the damage. I'd create a strong poker face and simply lose any emotion. Even today, I'm good at hiding my feelings—remnants from the days of my youth. When your world seems flipped and everything is so wrong, seemingly totally against you, all you do is go forward and live strong. You find a few tangible things, focus your energy on them, and hold on to them as if they were your rescue. I remember some nights it was so difficult that I hoped I would not wake up the next morning. But I kept waking up to reality every day.

ESCAPE

In 1989, when there were no cell phones, my home had a simple black phone with an attached cord hung on the wall, in a centralized location, so anyone in the house could hear your conversations. One night I sneaked out and went straight to a payphone so no one could hear the important call I needed to make.

I felt it was the most courageous call I ever made in my short life, and I dialed the numbers of the green public payphone carefully to ensure I got them correct. The number I dialed from memory was my maternal grandmother's. When my grandmother picked the call, I simply asked if my mother was there.

Since the divorce, I had sparse contact with my mom, usually only once a year or so. My heart pounded as I waited for my mom to come to the phone, but after a slight pause, my grandma told me she wasn't there and to call back in a few days. The waiting was long, but that's what I did, finally reaching her a few days later and hearing her "hello" into the receiver. All I remember telling my mom was, "I need to live with you." She was living in a different prefecture, about three hours away by train, but at the time that distance seemed like it was across the ocean.

We set up a secret meeting. I pretended to go to volleyball club practice after school, but instead took the train and met up with Mom. She came near where my father and I lived, but my father had no idea we were meeting up that day. I remember not being able to say much but noticing her shoelaces were different colors on the left and right and thinking that was a little odd. We decided to arrange the move. I don't know what happened afterward, but I remember some of the things.

I moved into my mom's successfully on June 9. The tears, fears, and anger, which had built up over the years, didn't seem to matter. My grandfather cried like a baby and begged me to not go.

My father manipulated my teacher, who asked me to his office and called me a traitor, saying I was selfish for not appreciating my father's sacrifice. My relatives contacted me and said I was ungrateful. My dad even disappeared for a while, although I think it was part of his plan to make me feel guilty, and we had to search to find him. My father was a town official in a small, rural town, and people there respected and believed him. No one would ever suspect what was happening in our home. Instead, they listened to my father, who presented himself as the loving, hardworking man trying his best to care for a rebelling, unappreciative child who wanted to move out and live with her mother instead of him.

To this day, I have no idea how and where I found the strength and courage to leave. I believe what drove me was the knowledge that if I didn't leave, the abuse would have continued and likely gotten worse. I shudder when I think of what life could have been if I stayed, especially when the sexual abuse was escalating day by day.

FIRST SUICIDE ATTEMPT

After I moved into my mom's house, all my anger and frustration led to a difficult relationship with my stepdad and my mom. I seemed to hold them responsible for all that had happened since my mom had left. Looking back, I believe it was my way of trying to recover from the trauma, and not knowing how. One day I was brave enough to tell my mom about all that had happened with my father. She knew my dad was capable of physical, verbal, and emotional abuse, but didn't believe he would also sexually abuse me. The next morning, she told me she and her husband decided I had made up the story. It hit me hard as if it were destroying every cell in my body.

Over the next few weeks, and many dwellings, I felt alone and devastated. The reality was that no one believed my story, and the truth was that my innocence, as a child and a woman, had been carelessly stolen. I had made myself most vulnerable, sharing the deeply personal accounts of what happened to me, to the people I thought loved me most, and they didn't believe me. I felt unworthy of anything and found nothing to look forward to.

I recalled my father explaining his suicide attempt during his college years; he made it sound like it was a heroic or cool thing. I didn't agree that it was cool, but I was so tired of my life and didn't think it was worth continuing to live. I found a small knife, put the blanket over me, and began to cut my wrist. However, for some reason, the knife was not sharp enough and only a tiny bit of blood resulted. It was certainly not enough to take my life. Still, I kept crying and trying to cut my wrist.

My mom was working a lot of hours, running her own small business, and seldom came home during business hours. For some reason, on that particular day, she returned because she had forgotten something and found me while I was trying to commit suicide. She screamed and took the knife away and started to cry, but I think I was crying harder. She was concerned and thought I was mentally ill, so she took me to see a counselor. After an evaluation, I was prescribed some kind of medication. I remember my first counselor was a male. He was sincere, but never really got to the heart of my problem, instead relying on medication to make my world right. I also remember that soothing, rather annoying music they played at the counselor's office, the white walls, and depressing atmosphere.

I despised taking the medicine. It made me less angry but more and more confused. I told my mom I wanted to cease counseling and stop taking the medicine. It wasn't helping. My mom couldn't understand why I had tried to commit suicide, but I certainly knew why. For me, it was just too difficult to live, especially when no one believed my true story.

JURI LOVE

REALIZING MY FULL POTENTIAL

It was during my second year of high school when I realized I completely hated school and myself. The pressure from this unsolved puzzle in my head seemed unbearable. Who I was, what I was, what happened to me, and why all of it gnawed at me and I just wanted to quit! I failed many subjects, got zeros on a math test, but I didn't care. Finally, I just stopped going to school. I simply lost the motivation to live another day.

One day, my friend suggested that I consider volunteering. I had no idea what that meant. The recommendation was to go to city hall and sign up as a volunteer to help disabled people. With little hope for myself and my future, I simply followed what my friend suggested.

I signed up for two nights at an overnight volunteer camp. I had no expectations. It was simply a means to quit high school. Still, my friend kept trying to keep me in school, telling me that without a high school diploma my choices in my future life would be limited. "You have one more year left, just try your hardest to finish," he said. Those words played in my head during this first volunteering experience.

I was assigned an adult male who had been wheelchair-bound since birth. I think he was in his midthirties. In addition to his physical handicap, he could not speak and used a hiragana (Japanese character) chart to point to letters spelling out what he needed. I remember his difficulty with just trying to tell me what he wanted to help me feed him. He pointed to に (ni), and in another few minutes, he pointed to く (ku). *Niku* means meat, so I brought him a small piece of beef to his mouth using a spoon. It would take over an hour to feed him.

After that, we went to a room that was a mix of other volunteers and disabled, where we had "conversation" time. My assigned person, whom I just helped to eat dinner, used his hiragana chart to start a sentence one letter at a time. It took almost ten minutes for him to complete a sentence.

"せんげつはつらかった (Last month was very hard)," he spelled out.

I had just met him and we couldn't communicate normally, so we shared nothing beyond the simple phrases he would point to. I had no idea why last month had been hard for him. He used ten more minutes to complete another sentence.

"ははがしんだ (My mother died)."

He didn't stop there. I watched him, as he slowly continued . . . He pointed to each letter to create words, yet I had no idea what his next sentence would be. I certainly held no insight that what this man would write would forever change my life and perspective.
He finished, and I somberly read:

"ぼくのせい (It was my fault)."

It was true I suffered through a difficult childhood, but watching this man point to letters to speak made me realize I have a fully functional body that I was taking for granted. I also realized I complained too much and needed to stop thinking everyone was my enemy. Finally, I determined that it was time to start believing in myself, that I was not living up to my full potential. This life-changing experience happened when I was seventeen, during a break between my junior and senior years in high school.

After he pointed out those telling words, I vowed to stop complaining and challenged myself to be the best I could be. This meant changing my mindset from the pessimistic, self-pitying person I had become, to one who always saw the glass as half full and never gave up. I became determined not to become a victim of my own making, wracked with guilt and regret. I would leave the old me behind and begin again.

MODELING AND STUDYING ABROAD

After this eye-opening experience, I opened up to new experiences and committed myself to never let thoughts of inferiority and the trauma from my past intervene and hinder me from achieving the goals I wanted to accomplish in my life.

I applied to a modeling audition for a major magazine in Tokyo. My friends said it was unlikely I would be chosen because I was not the prettiest in the school, but they were wrong. At age seventeen I began working as a fashion model in Tokyo, and I loved it very much. All the beautiful clothes I got to wear, makeup, photoshoots, seeing myself in the magazines—it was a surreal experience for sure.

Another life-changing experience was when I applied to an exchange student program in America through the city where I lived. The first time, I failed the exam, but on my second try, I passed and was sponsored by my city to travel to America for two weeks on scholarship. In total, eleven high school students from all over Japan were chosen. We all met in Tokyo before the flight to America. The students I met from the program were all so inspiring. I remain in contact with all of them, having found lifelong, inspirational friends through the program. We were greeted by the Japanese crown prince and princess at the emperor's palace. I remember the emperor's palace very well; I enjoyed super delicious orange juice, the likes of which I had never tasted in my life. I also remember the carpet we walked across was as soft as cotton balls.

After meeting with the crown prince and princess (who have now become the Japanese emperor and empress) and completing our training for the trip, I took the first flight in my life. After many hours in the air, I arrived in Seattle, Washington. My first impression of America was that it was big! Everything seemed so large—huge, I would say. People were also so generous. I fell in love with the country almost instantly. After the two-week program in America that summer, I decided to go back to America again, this time for a longer exchange program.

However, there were some obstacles to navigate that weren't so small. The program conflicted with my senior year of high school. My high school teacher in Japan told me if I attended classes every day and maintained the highest test scores, he would average out my grades for the last semester and allow me to graduate. To this date, I am still grateful for my sensei, who displayed so much faith in me and allowed me to graduate. Doing so required him to negotiate on my behalf to secure approval with the principal and vice principal of the high school.

The exchange program took me to a town in Washington called Burlington, where I stayed for six months. I was now eighteen. My host family was simply amazing. I cannot express enough gratitude to the Perry family, who made me feel like family, and Linda, the program coordinator and my first host mom for the two-week program. It was also through this program that I met another student who was selected by Nagoya, Japan: Natsuko, who would inspire me and become my best friend, forever.

I entered America as a senior at Burlington High School. I spoke no English and found it difficult to understand. For some reason, my school advisor thought mythology would be an easy course for me to take. Unfortunately, I had no idea what mythology was. I remember my host mother drawing a picture of strange snakes with three heads and having no idea what the class was trying to convey!

The other class I took was current events. Most of the time I had no idea what was going on. But especially, I had no idea what affirmative action was. Japan is a homogeneous society and such issues were not prevalent. My host father tried so hard to explain it to me, nearly every day. I remember my assignment was to read one page of *Time* magazine, and that was extremely hard. Additionally, I took physical education, music, and children's theater.

Despite the initial language issues and the cultural differences I needed to learn, I truly enjoyed being a student in America. I am still in touch with my lovely host family and the great friends I made in Washington. I became active in the exchange program, interfacing with other exchange students, participating in talent shows, volunteering at the senior center to play piano, and I did every fun thing I could during the beautiful six months of an exchange program. But my English skills were still bad. I remember one time some students told me they were going to Red Robin (a restaurant) after choir. I had no idea what they said, so I called my host mother and said, "I think we are going to Robin's house with everyone." It wasn't until after we drove to the destination that I found out it was a restaurant.

The American school system gave me many opportunities to thrive, and I fell in love with the country. I appreciate everyone who helped me get through my first American life experience and became my great friends.

MEETING ED LITTLE

While attending Burlington High School, I played piano as an accompanist for two choir classes, which I am still so grateful for. I thoroughly enjoyed being part of the choir and it afforded me many opportunities to meet other people. The most memorable and favorite part of the choir was that we took special trips to perform and compete. One was to Victoria Island in Canada, another was to San Francisco.

When we traveled to San Francisco, all the high school students were on a tour bus for three days. One day, when I was practicing the piano in the hotel lobby, I noticed our bus driver approach the piano to listen to me play. He began tearing up and shared with me that his wife also played the piano. She had died of cancer not long ago. His name was Ed Little. After listening to me play, he commented that I have a God-given talent. "Don't ever give up," he told me. He found such a place in my heart that when I returned to Washington, I wrote my first singer-songwriter composition, "Never Feel Alone." I recorded it on a cassette tape and sent it to Ed, which he told me later that he cherished for the rest of his life.

Little did I know then how much this encounter would influence my life.

We remained in touch since then, and he always impressed upon me how important it was that I never give up my music. Sadly, Ed passed away in 2013. He offered to adopt me (but I was too old) when I needed a visa to stay in America. He came to my concert when I was playing keyboard on a national tour with Kate Pierson (The B-52's), Graham Parker, and Bill Janovitz. He drove from Arizona, where he lived, to Los Angeles, California, for that concert. Ed told everyone he met there that I was his adopted granddaughter and he was so proud of me. Ed later remarried a

31

lovely woman, Joyce. He always wrote to me, when I was back in Japan, and we kept in contact after I returned to America. He is one of the few people who truly believed in me to the point that he was convinced I could be a professional musician, even when I questioned my abilities.

Ed was such a kind soul, managing an RV park in Phoenix, Arizona. He took me to the Grand Canyon whenever I visited. He once confided that when he met me, I was not smiling genuinely but what he called "fake smiling." Ed said he could detect sadness within me, despite my cheery outer appearance. He was a Native American (Cherokee) and a very proud man. Even years later, when I was still married and living in the Northeast, he would call me from Arizona whenever he heard the news of a snowstorm in the Boston area. Ed was my mentor, my American family, and the utmost supporter and cheerleader of my life and career. Ed influenced me so deeply. Even now, whenever I try to be kind to someone I just met, I recall his generosity and genuine love for people. Quite an impressive man, this random bus driver I met on a trip with my high school choir, and because of his encouragement, I am standing here doing music, helping others, and not having a fake smile on my face anymore.

The last time I talked to him on the phone was before he passed away. He told me, "I love you. I am very proud of you." They were the words he told me probably a hundred times since I first met him in San Francisco. As I think and write about this proud man and mentor, who had the most beautiful and purest soul, I can't stop my tears from falling. A simple man who gave his simple love and support to a random Japanese girl he met in San Francisco in 1995. Ed, you forever changed my life.

Ed passed away in his tiny RV home in Yuma, Arizona. He told me before he died, by Cherokee tradition, he would be an eagle after he passed away and would watch over me. I went to his memorial service and performed a song I wrote for him. On the way to the memorial service at the parking lot, an eagle was soaring above me. I knew without question it was Ed, making good on his promise to watch over me.

To Ed, I thank you for believing in me when no one else did. Thank you for listening to me and for allowing me to be important enough in your life to be proud of. Your caring and compassion completely touched my heart, and your wisdom gave me the strength to overcome many challenges and helped me stay on a musical path. Please rest in peace in heaven.

THE PERSPECTIVE I GAINED
AFTER BECOMING HOMELESS

My sister was waiting for me at the airport when I returned to Japan from my amazing six-month exchange program in America. Instead of a full-blown welcome home, I was told by my sister that my mother said I had to be independent. I could not come home.

As a result, I became homeless the day I returned from America. I was eighteen years old. On the first night, I stayed at a hotel located near my home, using the little savings I had accumulated from a part-time job I was doing before I went to America. I was with my best friend from the exchange program. I had hoped she would stay with me at my home for a bit, but now, suddenly, I had no home, so she had to stay at the hotel with me on the day we returned from America.

I will never forget that day and my complete shock, disbelief, and devastation. After that, for about three weeks, I had no money left and was completely homeless. I returned home, hoping Mom would relent, but she told me at eighteen, I needed to become completely independent. She had said this when I was younger, but I always thought she was joking. I knew now she was not.

When you're homeless, you do what you must to survive. Here is the list of things I did during that time:

- Stayed with my friends
- Slept with random men so I would have a place to stay overnight
- Stayed at an all-night night club
- Stayed at a twenty-four-hour restaurant that became rather sketchy between 3:00 a.m. and 6:00 a.m.
- Stayed overnight at a park, where I also witnessed sketchy people
- Spent a few nights just roaming around

During this time, I cried thousands of tears. I was alone and miserable. I became hopeless and was convinced my life sucked. The sad truth was it did! This was at a time before smartphones and internet searches, so I spent one hundred yen (about one dollar) and bought a part-time job listing magazine. I thought it may be a good idea to look for work somewhere like a resort hotel, to see if I could get a job that might also offer shelter and food.

Fortunately, I found some ads and used a public phone to call the number of a resort hotel. The owner, who picked up the phone, was very nice and asked me when I could start. I told him, "Tomorrow!" The next day, I took a train and the owner picked me up at the station. The resort turned out to be a beautiful, privately owned hotel, situated in a famous location in Japan. The city, Hakone, is famous for its views of Mount Fuji, Japan's tallest mountain. In an ironic twist, it was the same mountain I had glimpsed every day during my youth.

It was a great job, but I worked very hard. I woke up at 7:00 a.m. my first day and worked until 11:00 p.m. that night. This pace continued for about a month and a half. My goal was to save enough money for a down payment on a small apartment in Tokyo, so I could live independently. I was growing up quickly and felt much older than my eighteen years.

I came to enjoy my job and learned skills from this experience I use even today. My workday continued to start at 7:00 a.m., when I would help prepare breakfast in the resort's huge kitchen, with the owners and two other part-time staff, for about thirty guests. I was tasked with using long chopsticks called 菜箸 (*saibashi*) to remove the chalaza from the eggs. The chalaza is the mucus-like structure that connects the yolk and white and separating it was painstaking work. However, the result is a tender texture and a smooth, yellow scrambled egg. It woke me up immediately because removing the slimy chalaza requires extreme focus. I still remove the chalaza when I crack eggs as a reflex, having done it so many times.

At the resort, I would then help serve breakfast and clean up after. Later, at around 10:00 a.m., after all the guests checked out, I would work with the other staff to clean the rooms. We had to be thorough because after we were done, the owner came to inspect. If he found a strand of hair or piece of dust, he would display it for us neatly on a tissue, on the nightstand, with a light shining upon it. I became proficient at vacuuming quickly so he did not have to turn that light on to reveal the missed dust.

After lunch, I was allowed to take a quick power nap. During this time, I sometimes answered the phone to make a reservation, since it was before the concept of online booking. At 3:00 p.m. it was time to start preparations for dinner. I would find my way back to the kitchen and begin getting things ready for a 7:00 p.m.

dinner service for thirty guests. As you might imagine, the work and timing were intense and the timing needed to be precise. Some of my jobs included cutting off about a millimeter from the bottom of cherry tomatoes so they would not roll off the plate. I used a toothpick to devein about a hundred shrimp. I have become an expert and am super-fast at removing the thin, purple vein from shrimp with a toothpick. I also learned to cook complicated dishes of Japanese and French-fusion cuisine. Preparing full-course dinners for thirty people was intense, but a lot of fun and an adrenaline rush!

Seeing the guests enjoy their meals and hearing their accolades about our cooking was rewarding. Due to the number of compliments we received, the owners trusted us enough to allow us to prepare main dishes without oversight. This was very rare in Japan. I learned many cooking skills from this job and cook like an Iron Chef in the kitchen today. Friends who see me cook today tell me I look scary because I become intense and move super-fast. Then they tell me my food is excellent! After dinner was served at the resort, we cleaned the dishes and prepared the kitchen for the next day. Then it was off to bed around 11:00 p.m. to wake up at 7:00 a.m. the next morning and repeat the process.

I adored the owners of the resort. If you ever travel to Japan, I encourage you to visit this lovely family-owned resort hotel in Hakone, Japan. Should you go, when you enjoy eggs at breakfast, be sure to appreciate that there is no chalaza. At dinner, be assured the shrimp is fully deveined. Check out their website: kuranju.com.

My homeless experience was difficult and stressful, but when I look back now, it was also impactful in a positive way. It gave me a lot of self-confidence, made me independent, and instilled in me the belief that no matter what happens, I can overcome, living my life up, making new friends, finding a job, and just being okay.

In retrospect, I guess I should appreciate my mother's tough-love philosophy for making me an independent, resilient, appreciative, humble, and positive person. People who meet me and have come to know me always say I possess these qualities. Certainly, my homeless experience helped shape those characteristics in me.

I would not wish for anyone to experience homelessness, but if you ever happen to become homeless, know there is another side from which you can emerge a better, stronger version of yourself. Can you imagine being homeless at eighteen? What would you have done differently if you were in that situation?

LIVING INDEPENDENTLY IN TOKYO

After I left Hakone with some money I earned from working at the resort, I returned to Tokyo. I rented my first tiny apartment on the outskirts of Tokyo in the town of Kanamachi. My first apartment was probably about four hundred square feet, with the tiniest kitchen containing one small electric stove and a ladder to a loft where I slept. It was about a twenty-minute walk from the nearest train station. I had little extra money to buy a real bed or comforter, so I bought a thirty-dollar sleeping bag to serve that purpose. When the temperature dropped and I got cold, I'd put a coat over the sleeping bag to add another layer of warmth. I was too proud of my small apartment and myself for living independently at nineteen regardless of my sleeping situation. (I at least had a roof above my head!) One thing I remember vividly and that I despised was battling the insects. Occasionally, a cockroach would fly up to the loft where I slept. I shrieked and thought I was going to die. When he landed, I would bravely pour detergent on him and watch him die. It was not all fun to live alone at that age, despite winning the gross cockroach battle. (I had no idea they could fly up to the loft!)

I perused the job listing magazine again, hoping to find a position where I could use and improve my English skills. I found a company based in the US that was looking for a sales associate, so I applied for the job. Thinking back, it was one of the sketchiest jobs I have ever done. The job was 100 percent commission based, selling products such as potpourri, watches with five different bands, calculators, and numerous miscellaneous items. The company was MLM (multilevel marketing) door-to-door sales. I would carry large boxes of items on the train, then solicit random businesses to see if I could leave samples and an order list for a few days, to be collected later in that week. Early in the week, I would go door to door to businesses in Tokyo, hoping to make sales. I knocked on every door and got rejected most of the time. It was a difficult job and I shed many tears that first week after I only made thirty dollars in sales. Despite working from 8:00 a.m. to 10:00 p.m. five days a week, I was so poor I would beg for food at a fish store at the end of the night, hoping there was a dish that hadn't sold that day that could be donated to me. Fortunately, the generous owner usually found something for me to eat.

One time I went into one building without realizing how dangerous it was. When I entered, I was immediately surrounded by a group of scary-looking Japanese men. I thought for sure they were going to kill me, but instead, they asked why I entered their building. I told them I was a salesperson, selling things like nice-smelling potpourri. Believe it or not, they bought one but told me never to enter the building again.

I found out later I had entered a yakuza office! The yakuza is the equivalent of a big gang. It is a Japanese mafia. I am sure you may have seen some yakuza movies. Looking back, I was fortunate to have escaped the encounter peacefully. And . . . I made a sale! Despite the reputation of the yakuza, the head guy gave me advice I still remember.

He said, "お姉ちゃん (Oneechan, which means older sister or young girl), sit down and look into my eyes." I did so out of fear— I was surrounded by at least five scary men who all crossed their arms and stared at me. He continued, "Have you ever heard the expression that your eyes are a window of your soul?" to which I replied, "No, sir." To this, he said, "You have such wise eyes. I can tell if you wanted to, you could even attend Tokyo University!" This was telling because Tokyo University is one of the best universities in Japan.

I will never forget that yakuza boss's compliment and the fact he was nice enough to have a small conversation with me, having some faith in my intelligence (though I never tried to enroll at Tokyo University) in addition to buying my one-thousand-yen (about ten dollars) potpourri. Still, it's frightening to think I went to a yakuza office to sell my wares.

As a nineteen-year-old salesperson, I struggled at selling. There was a lot of pressure to sell and to make any money on commission, and I had to sell a lot. One time, in my haste to sell, I fell down half a flight of stairs, spilling my samples everywhere. It was painful, and with no one to help, I needed to pick it all up and keep selling to put food on my table so that I didn't have to go back to the fish store to beg for leftover food. I kept at it, and with persevering, I got better, and I was promoted to a trainer. This was good and bad. It was a better job, but all of a sudden I had several trainees working under me. For a nineteen-year-old, it was a lot of pressure, because my commission was tied in with that of my trainees, as was theirs. So, several commissions were directly tied to my training, attitude, and combined performance. Most of the trainees were older men, probably in their thirties or forties. Some had children and families, which put more pressure on them, which in turn put more pressure on me.

My salary skyrocketed to about a thousand dollars a week in six months, a huge improvement from the thirty dollars a week where I had started. But a strange thing started to happen to me. Every time I looked at someone, I saw them simply as a potential sale. It made me feel dirty, like I was taking advantage of people. I remember thinking that happiness cannot be in proportion to the amount of the money you make, especially when doing something you truly do not love. At this time, most of my friends were still in college and getting financial support from their parents and enjoying their college experience. Some for sure were partying. I was jealous of them, especially when I'd see them laughing and having fun while I was carrying my wares and selling them around Tokyo. I shared these feelings with my boss and confided in her that the pressure was getting to me. I think she realized I was becoming depressed and was very kind to let me leave quietly one day without telling anyone I had left.

While it was a relief to leave that job, I felt pressure of a different kind. I felt like a loser and found myself depressed about not being able to cut it in the working world. I cried myself out, and one day, at wits' end, I visited the owner of the resort hotel where I used to work. I broke down in front of the owner, crying like a baby and sobbing about what a failure I was.

Without sympathy, but in a caring tone, he asked me, "Why are you crying?"

I looked at him, confused. He continued, asking a second question: "Wasn't that your choice to work there and also to quit?"

The question completely stopped my crying and made me realize that yes, it was my choice! It was a simple realization, but a powerful one. I still abide by his philosophy.

Yes, just about everything is *by our choice*. So why complain? If you don't like your situation, you have the power and a precious human right called "choice" to exercise control over it. It was some of the best advice I have ever received. Despite the stress and difficulty of a full-commission job, it did teach me some important lessons for the workplace.

First: Never display your emotions outwardly to coworkers and clients. Keep a calm demeanor at all times.

Second: Don't forget the "law of averages." Once, my boss gave this example using a deck of cards. He inserted a joker and flipped through the deck until we turned to the joker. Sometimes the joker appeared on the first flip, and sometimes you didn't see it until you flipped to the very last card. Many times, it was found in the middle. Likewise, in business, some days you sell a lot and some days you don't sell at all, but it averages out. In the end, the outcome is the same. The lesson is to be patient and put the same energy into everything you do. If you don't sell, it only means the cards you're flipping haven't revealed the joker yet. If you stop, however, the joker will never appear. So don't panic, and be consistent at what you do. The joker will eventually appear.

CHANGING MY LIFE COURSE

After quitting my commission job, I was unsure about what I would do next. One night I contracted food poisoning. I was alone in my apartment and couldn't recall which number to call for an ambulance (in Japan, police and medical emergency use a different number). I was in tremendous pain and didn't know what to do. I was rolling on the floor alone, thinking maybe I would die (I know now food poisoning is not likely to kill you). I started to think about all the things I would miss and some I had wanted to try. For some reason, my friend Ed's words came to me. I remembered what he wrote to me in one of his letters: "Don't ever give up on your music!"

Since leaving home, I had no longer played the piano. First, being homeless for a while, I didn't have one, and then when I lived in an apartment, I couldn't afford one. Additionally, I no longer had the desire to pursue my music career after returning from America given the severity of my situation. It was interesting how when I got sick, Ed's encouraging words came to my head: "You have a God-given talent!" He had told me this so many times it must have been engraved into my subconscious.

I suddenly realized if I did not return to America to study music, I would regret it for the rest of my life. So, after I recovered from my stomach ailment, I went to a resource center in Tokyo and found information about the Berklee College of Music. Berklee is a much-respected music college in Boston, Massachusetts. I discovered there was an upcoming scholarship tour I could audition for.

Shortly after my stomach incident, I found a job. Nothing crazy like my door-to-door commission job, but a position at one of the best hotels in Japan. The Hotel Okura in Tokyo was ranked five stars. My job was to be a laundry service operator. All the world-class stars came and stayed at Hotel Okura. Since most of the guests were English speaking, I was able to use my English a lot. Some of the famous people who stayed at the hotel and with whom I had some level of contact were former US presidents, foreign politicians, millionaires, James Cameron and Linda Hamilton, Sigourney Weaver, Rowan Atkinson (a.k.a. Mr. Bean), and Yoko Ono. My favorite was Björk! I got to take their phone calls about picking their laundry up and I would ask about their laundry needs, where to find the washing, and where to return it. I had to say, "Would you please leave them on the bed, sir?" a million times. Or I had to call and inform the celebrity that we could not dry-clean that particular material.

While working there, I started to seriously focus on saving

money for my study abroad. I only spent for my basic needs: food, minimal clothes, and rent. Everything else I put toward my education. It was a fun job, taking laundry orders from the customers and directing the delivery girls to the rooms they needed to go to. It was a large hotel, with a staff of about four thousand. I started as part time, but after working for about two years, they offered me a full-time position. Given the Hotel Okura's reputation as one of the best hotels in Japan, most people would have jumped at this opportunity, but my goal was to return to America to study music. I politely declined. All in all, I ended up saving about $30,000 during the two and a half years I worked at the hotel. I was proud of myself, especially when I had no financial help from anyone.

One day, in Tokyo, I auditioned for a scholarship to attend the Berklee College of Music in Boston. I arrived at the audition wearing a kimono and was asked by the school staff if I was attending a summer festival or ceremony following the audition. I told them, "No, I wore kimono for this audition so I can be remembered!" He smiled and told me I'd do well at Berklee if I won the scholarship. At the end of the day, I did succeed in winning a partial scholarship to Berklee, and as predicted, I did well at the school.

Unfortunately, while working at the hotel, some of my coworkers started to bully me. This occurred after the big bosses left and there was less supervision. They started by calling me names, but it escalated and seemed to get worse day by day. When I look back, I think these people were jealous, because they knew I was going to America.

One day I had enough and decided it had to end then and there. I sought out the person who had bullied me the most and looked her in her face.

"Do you think you were born to bully me?" I asked her. "What is the mission of your life? Which direction are you going in your precious life?"

She said nothing, just stared at the wall for a long time. After that day, she never bullied me again. She became very nice to me, which I found rather bizarre.

It can be as simple as standing up for yourself to repress the attitude of bullies.

Sometimes, I think people bully for attention. Perhaps by putting her in her place, I was able to help her realize she should focus on her life rather than pick on one individual who couldn't change her life in the end.

Other than the bullying part, I enjoyed working at the Hotel Okura. I learned real manners and how to speak politely. For instance, "Hai" is "Yes" in Japanese, but the hotel insisted I use the politest version of "Yes," which is, "Sayoude gozaimasuka." Not many people commonly use this phrase, but when a customer is picking up their laundry and you say, "Sayoude gozaimasuka," you can be sure they notice.

I was grateful for all the hotel did in helping me refine my Japanese and English language skills and in training me to provide exceptional and world-class customer service.

WINNING AN EMPLOYEE SPEECH CONTEST

As I've mentioned, when I was working at Hotel Okura, I tried to save everything I could for my studies in America at the Berklee College of Music. I didn't have extra money to take English lessons, which I desired. However, the Hotel Okura offered English-language contests to help improve the utilization of spoken English. Being a part-time employee, I was not allowed to participate. It took some doing, but eventually, I negotiated my way into the contest. In my first year, I came in second place, but the next year, I won the contest. I was so proud as my name, speech, and an award were published in the employee magazine for about four thousand employees to read.

I want to share the speech I gave that won me the English Speech Contest. It was written when I was twenty-one years old and working in Tokyo for the Hotel Okura. I memorized the entire speech and received many compliments.

"A Genuine Smile"

How many people are conscious of their existence?

People have inherited the baton of life from their ancestors. But the time we can live is limited and no one knows the limit of their own life. I read once that a woman has the potential to give birth to the future, but a man doesn't have that same potential. And that is why men work especially hard to create something while they are living. Even though we live and struggle hard through trial and error, our lifespan is a mere moment in time, especially if you consider the long history of earth and space.

This brings me to the question of why people live trying with all their might to search for their existence. I've heard that "the person who carries a fully scheduled diary, also carries an empty head," particularly in a big city.

In ancient times, people had no measurement of time. They lived each moment as it came. However, for convenience's sake, "time" as we know it was made. Now in the present day, we're losing the real meaning of "time," and even more, our reason for being. Time gives us the illusion that we can never actually catch the moment. The moment is always passing us by. Such being the case, it is no easy thing to search for the real meaning of "life."

I wonder how many people honestly feel like they are completely living when they make an effort to look at themselves in the mirror each day. And this makes me think that the meaning of a genuine smile is that the real smile can only come from the person who knows what kind of person they are and what is the most important thing in their life and what their aim in life is. We need to face ourselves and also to endeavor to have a genuine smile. That is why the genuine smile is so worthwhile and beautiful.

Our smile shouldn't depend on our emotions or mood for that day. It only comes from the person who knows their existence and feels like they're completely living. In conclusion, I know it is hard to think like this, but wouldn't it be nice if we could find the real meaning of our lives?

Thank you for giving me this opportunity to speak to you today.

A LITTLE SETBACK

One of the perks of working at the Hotel Okura was the routine medical check-ups they offered for all the employees. I went for my physical thinking nothing of it, but when the doctor checked my throat, he told me I required further testing. I was also asked to make an appointment for a blood test. The diagnosis came back that I had a hyperthyroid disease. I was given prescription medication but suffered an awful reaction to it. The doctor then told me they had to remove my thyroid. I was shocked, as I suffered no symptoms.

I received my scholarship acceptance letter from the Berklee College of Music for the fall semester, starting in September of 1997. But because of my thyroid disease, I had to defer my enrollment for a year. At the time it was devastating, but in the end, it worked out for the best, because I was able to save more money. I ended up spending my birthday, September 3, in the hospital. I spent a total of two weeks there—one week before and one week after the operation. The operation was so difficult, but the prognosis from the doctor who performed the surgery was even worse. No, it was totally cruel.

He bluntly told me, "You will have a scar on your neck. You may contract the disease again, requiring radiation, which is likely to prevent you from becoming pregnant. Most men want families, so no men will want to marry you. I don't care because I am going to America soon." I should have reported this heartless doctor, but I was too naïve back then and didn't say anything. That would not be the case today.

On the day of the operation, they administered several local shots on my neck to numb the surgical area. The needles were incredibly painful, but that was not the worst part of the surgery. The most painful aspect was that they could only partially anesthetize me because they needed to see my vocal cord while removing the partial organ of the thyroid. I had to say, "Ah . . ." to stimulate the vocal cord and keep it visible throughout the surgery. I remained semiconscious throughout the operation, an awful experience. Today I'm still sensitive whenever someone comes close to touching my neck—I will jump. When the operation was over, I had lost 70 percent of my thyroid. During my surgery, I could hear the doctors bickering about things that were unrelated to my operation. It was upsetting and I wanted to scream, but of course, I could not. Two nurses were holding my hands and I squeezed their hands back the whole time. I was blindly held with a white towel but could see the light bleeding through, hear everything, and smell the burn.

On my left side was who I assumed was the MD and on my right side may have been a resident. The MD was yelling at the resident, "Don't hold the needle on the windpipe. You are always talking about girls and food, and that's why the patient had to suffer more minutes on the operation table." I was scared, but of course, I could not do anything while my neck was cut open.

After the surgery, I ended up losing my voice for an entire month, maybe due to vomiting violently during my recovery. Looking back, I would have done things much differently now, including litigation against the doctor who harassed me. Between having to defer my enrollment at Berklee, the difficult surgery, and harassment by the medical doctors, it was another really strenuous time in my life. But I appreciated all of my friends who visited me at the hospital and gave me lots of gifts, well-wishes, and encouragement.

CHAPTER 3

From Homeless to Berklee College of Music

I REMEMBER THE EXCITEMENT OF FLYING TO BOSTON, Massachusetts, in September of 1998. I had worked so hard to save money and waited so long for this trip to happen. I remember getting up early to catch the first train for the airport. All the frustration and difficulties of the past year melted in the skyline from the small window of the airplane. It had been such a long journey to get to this moment, but now that I was airborne, I felt every endured struggle—being abused, homeless, bullied, and humiliated—all passing far below me. I recall such a sense of release, knowing I was headed toward a brand-new life in America.

It was love at first sight from the first day I arrived in Boston to attend the Berklee College of Music. I rented a small apartment, about twenty minutes away from the college by train. It was my first time living in America on my own, and it was very exciting.

One thing I did immediately after starting my classes was to review my budget. I divided my tuition down to the minute and determined the cost to be about three dollars per minute during the class. Knowing I was spending my hard-earned money from many hours worked at the Hotel Okura, I was determined not to waste a dime (yen). I was a focused student who attended many of the professors' office-hour sessions, worked with a tutor, and participated in every concert and jam session. I was in heaven playing music all day, learning a lot, and meeting amazing musicians from all over the world.

Compared to some of the students' musical backgrounds, I felt somewhat at a disadvantage. I began my classical piano lessons at the age of three but quit when I was seventeen, so I never got into all of the theoretical nuances of music. I possessed no real knowledge of jazz, chord charting, arranging other instruments, and playing in a large ensemble. I learned so much about music at Berklee. Every day was super busy, packed with wonderful classes, rehearsals, recording sessions, homework, practice, and playing in the concerts. I slept only an average of four hours a night during the college year. It was an incredible experience and I made so many inspiring, lifelong friends during my time there.

Many of the teachers and friends I met at Berklee, from all over the world, are still my motivation. Everyone I know is doing well after graduation. I hold my decision to attend Berklee as one of the best decisions I have ever made in my life. I wanted to stand out from other students, so at all the big concerts, I wore colorful wigs, angel wings, and sometimes Christmas lights. The lights turned out not to be such a good idea, as they burned my skin a little on the stage.

Attending the Berklee College of Music gave me great confidence in myself as a musician. I also came to appreciate how diverse music is, and beyond the music, something about the diversity of human beings. I cannot thank enough all of the teachers and mentors I met at Berklee for their wisdom, and all of the amazing friends I made during the experience. Hopefully, they know who they are and that my sincere admiration and love go out to each of them.

WISDOM FROM LEE BERK, A FORMER PRESIDENT OF BERKLEE

One of the highlights of attending Berklee was meeting Lee Berk, the music school's former president. The Berklee College of Music was named after him (flip the last name and first name) when first founded by his father. Now Berklee is considered one of the best music colleges in the world.

Lee offered me the opportunity to help coordinate a public concert event through the school. I was part of a team that auditioned bands and selected the top ten to perform at the Hynes Convention Center for a career expo. While it turned out a big success, I was stressed working through all the details in putting together such an event. I still remember Lee coaching me, "Juri, you are focused on the result, but the process is one of the most important things. You can enjoy the process, not only the result."

This simple wisdom still lives within me. Now every time I'm in a similar situation, I recall his words and enjoy the process. As a result, I can watch how it grows and be more a part of it, instead of panicking and worrying about the outcome.

Many accomplished Japanese musicians have graduated from the Berklee College of Music, and for his dedication to that cause, Mr. Berk was honored by the Japanese emperor. He received an honorary medal on behalf of the emperor at the Japanese consulate general's house in Boston. I was asked to speak about my experience at Berklee and the influence the college and Mr. Berk made on my life. It was a special day, and I was extremely humbled to participate in this ceremony and share in Lee Berk's accomplishment. It was especially gratifying for me, knowing how I came to Berklee on my own.

Lee and Susan Berk are an amazing couple. Lee has been kind enough to mentor me over the years, even after his retirement. I feel privileged and honored to call Lee Berk my mentor.

A TRIP TO GHANA

My experiences at Berklee were not limited to learning music at the campus. One great trip that I took with other Berklee students and our professor was to Ghana, Africa. We learned how to play African drums and perform African dances in four different cities in Ghana. On some days, it was a total music experience, playing and learning music from 9 a.m. to 5 p.m. Some areas we visited had neither electricity nor running water. It was a tremendous, once-in-a-lifetime experience. I was proposed to nine times during our three-week visit, and I refused them all. Here are two of the most ridiculous marriage proposals: One, I was swimming in the ocean and this Ghanaian guy swam toward me and said, "Will you marry me?" I was swimming also and said no. It would be funny if I had said yes to the random swimmer, who to this day I have no idea what his name was.

The second time happened when we were departing the country. The security guy at the airport checked out my passport and stared it for a long time. I thought I was in trouble and started to get nervous.

"When are you coming back to Ghana?" he asked.

I said, "I don't know."

He then closed my passport after the examination and said, "Will you marry me?"

I said no and got on the airplane back to Boston.

One tribe chief we met in Tamale had five wives. He was sixty-four years old and his fifth wife was only twenty-two. When I asked the wives if they were jealous of one another, they all said no, they were happy to be married to a chief. Such a different culture.

One day, we ordered drums, and two goats were killed for their skins. It was eye-opening and made me appreciate all instruments after that.

My time in Ghana was probably the most intense three weeks of my life. I always wanted to visit Africa, ever since meeting a wonderful musician in Tokyo from the Democratic Republic of the Congo. He introduced me to some wonderful African music while I was in Japan. It was part of my dream to not only visit America, but also Africa to study music. I composed many songs while interacting with my Ghanian teachers, who were young, focused, and knowledgeable. Some of my teachers were young boys, but their intensity toward playing music completely changed the way I approached performing. My stance, the way I held the instrument, my breathing, channeling my focus into the music, the ability to isolate myself from all the background noise—all came from their tutelage. I truly had an amazing time in Ghana. I asked one of the music masters, "How can I make music people will like?"

He touched my forehead and my heart and told me, "Your heart must connect to your brain, and you must love your music. People won't love your music if you don't."

It was another of those moments when you know wisdom is being shared. I try my best to exercise that insight whenever I compose, perform, or teach music. If you love your creation and art first, the rest of the world will follow your passion.

FINISHING MY DEGREE

Before starting the last semester of my associate degree, I ran out of money to pay the tuition. I only needed a few credits to finish my degree, so I needed less than $3,000 with my scholarship. I bought the cheapest airline ticket and returned to Japan. I found a job right away working at an *izakaya*, a bar-type restaurant that serves delicious Japanese tapas. I worked from 6 p.m. to 6 a.m. every day, also taking every other shift that became available. I also took on a second job as a supervisor for students taking tests at a learning center, from 8 a.m. to 12 p.m. Then, I would sleep for about four hours and return to the *izakaya* for my next day shift. I maintained this crazy schedule for about a month before I earned enough money to cover the remaining amount of my tuition. I graduated from the Berklee College of Music with an associate degree in 2001.

Upon graduation, I started to work as a musician, teaching piano and voice to several students. Mostly I gave private lessons and did gigs, playing the piano in bands, and solo for parties, weddings, funerals, political events. You name it, I probably played it. I also made a few albums of my own and performed on other musicians' albums as a keyboardist/pianist. I enjoyed working as a musician and performing on many occasions.

In 2003 I got an amazing opportunity to do a national tour as the keyboard player for a project band composing an album called *Lost Songs of Lennon and McCartney*. As the name implies, the album featured all the songs John Lennon and Paul McCartney wrote for other artists. Some of the artists on the album included Kate Pierson of The B-52's, Bill Janovitz, and Graham Parker. The album's producer was Jim Sampas. I was hired two days before the start of rehearsal for the national tour. In addition to keyboards, I also was a backup singer and played the melodica. We toured all over the United States and I enjoyed the time of my life. I was extremely honored to share a stage with these legends and incredible musicians—Marc Copely, Winston Roye, and Joe Magistro, to name a few. I loved everyone on our tour. Kate and I still talk, and she kindly invites me backstage every time she is in town with The B-52's.

A rock-star moment from this national tour happened when I was in Hollywood, California. I had met up with some friends and was exiting a restaurant on Hollywood Boulevard. Suddenly a tiny Asian man inserted himself between my friend and me and punched her stomach before elbowing me. I was shocked as he ran off with no explanation or words exchanged. People gathered around us and asked if we were okay. It hurt, but it was not life-threatening. I told people, "I have a six-pack, so I am okay!" And I do.

The next day, I told the band about my experience. They were stunned and felt bad for me. Our tour manager in particular be-came worried about me. I managed the next night's performance in San Diego with a little bit of pain but knew the show must go on. After our show, one hotel room got double-booked. As a cour-tesy, the hotel gave us a penthouse suite. Everyone felt so bad for me that the tour manager decided to give me that gorgeous pent-house room. I felt like I had won the lottery. Instead of all these legends, I got to stay in the biggest room in the hotel with an amazing view of downtown San Diego. Everyone said, "Juri, you are a true rock star!"

I loved performing in front of the huge crowd every night. I would love to be able to do that for the rest of my life.

In 2010, I went back to Berklee College of Music to finish my bachelor's degree. At the time, I was going through separation and divorce from my first husband. I was taking twelve credits per semester, across two semesters, to finish my degree. These were mainly academic classes and some music history.

At the time, I was also running a nonprofit organization, playing piano for a musical, teaching private lessons, and was pregnant with my first child, from my boyfriend, who would later become my second ex-husband. My first pregnancy was not complicated but featured lots of morning sickness throughout. The final week of the semester was the tech and production week of the musical *Annie Get Your Gun*. I was at the rehearsal for the musical while trying to memorize terminology for the test. I learned hardcore time management throughout this experience. I employed a timer and a to-do-list to stay focused and isolate me from distraction.

I remember one of my final test mornings I vomited standing up at the café where I was trying to get breakfast, and I had to call my professor to please reschedule the test for the final. She generously did, and I was able to get a 97 on the rescheduled test. When I got my final grades, they were all As and my GPA was 4.0. I was very proud of myself.

CHAPTER 4

Founding
Genuine Voices

IN MY ORIGINAL ACADEMIC PLAN, SEPTEMBER 2001 WAS
the beginning of my last semester at Berklee, and I was required
to do a senior project of my major, called Professional Music
Major. Most of the students performed a recording or concert for
their senior project upon graduation. I endeavored to do something different, something involving community service. As I considered what I might do, I was reading a Japanese book that spoke
of a man who taught journalism in juvenile detention centers in
California. The story focused on one of his students who became
a professional screenwriter in Hollywood. It felt like a thunder-
bolt running through my spine when I read this, and I knew I had
found my inspiration and wanted to do a similar type of project.
I thought about youth in a jail cell, who cannot go anywhere, and
what a laptop to create music might do to open their world and
escape from reality for a bit. That was a little idea that began in-
cubating in my mind.

Then, on the eleventh of September 2001, the whole world was
shocked by the terrorist attacks. This motivated me even more to

make this world a better and more peaceful place, and I became determined to create something meaningful. I had countless meetings with my advisors and community members about how I might bring my idea to fruition.

One of the first advisors I spoke with was Mr. Spellman, who became my role model and mentor later in life. At the time, he was the director of the Career Development Center at Berklee College of Music. I went to seek his wisdom and share the small yet clear vision in my head. He told me my idea of teaching music in detention centers sounded like the impetus for a nonprofit organization. I was puzzled by that term because I had never heard of it. I then started to research nonprofit organizations and formed Genuine Voices on October 31, 2002. I had absolutely no idea about running a nonprofit, but I had the passion and asked around for advice, which I received from many people. I must say, I was fortunate that people trusted me and truly supported me from the beginning. It is another reason I love America. When you have the passion and an idea for a good cause, people do not discriminate nor discourage you.

I ran Genuine Voices as president and founder for twelve years until 2014. I have met many incredible people through Genuine Voices, and we impacted many lives through teaching music in detention centers. I hired over two hundred volunteers and interns during those twelve years to sustain the program and did so with a minimal budget. I stumbled my way through in the beginning, but again, I wasn't shy about asking good questions. Being humble and appreciative went a long way in gaining the support of people who were willing to help transform this idea into a life-changing organization.

And life-changing it was, for a number of the young people we taught music to in those detention programs have found the course of their lives completely transformed. Even a little "Twinkle Twinkle Little Star" we taught on the piano or guitar led to a full-length CD we had created with the youth. Many had not only learned musical skills, but also gained a sense of ownership, self-esteem, and confidence.

I cannot be prouder to have started Genuine Voices, and am amazed to think how it originated, became a reality, and changed lives, sprouting from a tiny idea inspired by a book I read in my small studio apartment in Boston.

BOYS AND GIRLS CLUB

I wasn't sure how to get my idea started at the beginning. One of the first actions I took was to search "kids in jail," in the hopes I'd find something to build from. A probation officer came up in the results. He was involved with youth crime prevention work in the Dorchester District Court in Boston. I immediately called him and asked if he would meet with me. He graciously agreed to meet a few days later. I remember taking the train (Red Line) and walking to his office. I was nervous about what would happen next and what would result from this meeting. Of course, I went there alone, and I was a bit intimidated by the atmosphere. Despite my trepidation, he welcomed me with a big smile and was very nice. Not wishing to waste his time, I told him straight away that I wanted to help youth in detention centers by teaching music and music productions. He kindly suggested that since I am Japanese, and know nothing about gangs, gang violence, and crimes in America, I should try to start my program with at-risk youth instead of those already in detention programs and focus on preventing the violence. At the time I had no idea what that meant, but he provided a list of locations in low-income areas with high crime rates and told me it would be great if my music program could impact those communities.

Next, I needed to locate musical instruments for the program. Fortunately, simply asking the many people I knew at Berklee resulted in success. Mr. Mash, the founding chair of the music synthesis department at Berklee, decided to donate a laptop, speaker, keyboard, and software named Reason, a cool beat-making program. I was so grateful to receive this generous donation.

I also went to the Community Government Affairs Office at my college to solicit help to realize my idea. They were excellent. After visiting two sites, we selected the Boys and Girls Club of Dorchester, Massachusetts, as the pilot for our music program. There was no music program in place to begin with, so it was difficult for people to grasp the concept. Nonetheless, they were excited about the idea and were supportive.

I began with six students in a tiny closet room that was used as a music lesson space. With our single keyboard, small speakers, and laptop, along with three volunteer teachers and myself in 2001, I orchestrated the program until 2003. By then there were about two hundred students in the program taking music lessons. The Community Government Affairs Office also tapped into federal government funding to create an off-campus work-study program, so some eligible students (they had to be US citizens and on financial aid) could work as music teachers as part of the program.

Today, the program is still going strong and has won an award as the best music program in the Boys and Girls Clubs of America. The program provides free music lessons to an average of six hundred at-risk youth. In 2009, one donor generously donated $100,000 to construct a recording studio and music space and funded a full-time music teacher position. I am so grateful to everyone involved in this project. Many individuals worked hard for these students to make the program a resounding success. In 2009, I was honored at the opening ceremony of the studio for initiating the program. When I started it was just a closet space, but since those early days, some walls were removed and now half the floor is dedicated to the music program.

The last time I visited the Boys and Girls Club in Dorchester was with a Japanese TV crew when they were filming a documentary about my life. That was in October 2016 (the show aired in March 2017 with an official rating of 7.5 million viewers). When I arrived on the music floor with the TV crew, the atmosphere was so vibrant, the air was filled with beautiful music throughout. I couldn't help but cry. I was just so incredibly proud to have initiated the program, and immensely happy to see these kids beaming, taking pride in themselves and their music, smiling, and making music together.

I met one young man who was practicing the drums in a soundproof practice space that had some drum sets. He was sixteen at the time and was clearly an extremely talented drummer. The TV crew interviewed him. He told us his father had just passed away, a victim of gun violence. His father had been working on his car in front of their house and a stray bullet found him. He was an innocent victim of gang war and street violence. I could not help but cry for this young boy's loss and the responsibility ahead now that he had lost his father.

He told me his father loved his drumming and believed he would be a star someday. I told him in my eyes, he was already a star. He also mentioned that the Boys and Girls Club had been his oasis since he was a young boy. Even on the day after his father passed away, he came to practice his drums. I was so touched by his story. Hearing his story and others like it was such a testimony to this program, made possible by the generosity and support of many people. I have become good friends with this young man and can say that beyond his amazing musical ability, he is an equally incredible human being. He is humble and smart, in addition to his aforementioned talent. He thanked me profusely for starting the music program. It was certainly worth it after hearing his appreciation and seeing his love of music, and others like him who have benefitted from the program. The young man I speak of is Dashawn, and I have no doubt he will be successful in his musical endeavors, as well as in life. I love you, Dashawn, and I am so proud of you!

In 2012, I was featured on a Channel 4 television segment in Boston. When the probation officer I had met with was interviewed by Channel 4, he stated: "Juri came to our community and replaced the sound of gunfire with the sound of music." I could not be prouder. In one of the many meetings I had with the probation officer, when I was running Genuine Voices and had told him I want to save many lives and help the world, he shared some very important wisdom with me. He told me, "Juri, focus on changing one person at a time. If you can change one youth to a positive life pattern, that youth will come back to the community as a positive influence. It will create a ripple effect and eventually be able to change the world." I never forgot his philosophy, and I have always applied it and focused on changing one youth at a time.

DETENTION CENTER

Even though I was able to start a successful music program at the Boys and Girls Club, I still had a passion to teach music in the detention program. One day I was introduced to an education director at one of the detention programs in Boston and was able to get the program underway at one of the centers. I was supported by Berklee College of Music, in the form of a $5,000 Alumni Endowment Grant. My mentor, Lee Berk, the president of Berklee

College of Music, emailed me when it was initiated by the board and encouraged me to apply. I was the first recipient among three other alumni. With the funding, I was able to pay for teachers and purchase equipment for the program. From this small start, over the next twelve years, Genuine Voices provided music lessons in seven detention centers across Massachusetts and two after-school programs in Washington (where I had been an exchange student when I was eighteen years old). I was so fortunate to have the help of many wonderfully talented volunteers and interns, who worked tirelessly to make the music program possible. Additionally, I enjoyed the support of countless donors and foundations who supported our mission. For this, I am eternally grateful. Particularly, I am grateful for the Lenny Zakim Fund, which supported our program for three consecutive years, not only helping to fund the program but also by providing extensive training for the recipients of their generous grant.

The whole experience was life-changing, not just for me but for almost everyone who participated in the program. We all found the program challenging but extremely rewarding. It is not easy to teach a population whom society has labeled as "criminals." Most, I would come to believe, were victims themselves, and were incarcerated for reasons that were rooted in our society's failure and responsibility. It is difficult to grow up as a contributing member of society when you have zero positive role models and no environment to correct your path to remain productive and positive when you go astray. And to be honest, I could easily have been one of the incarcerated youth in Japan after having gone through my difficult times at home, and that is one of the strongest reasons I had a tremendous amount of passion and compassion for this particular population.

One boy, whom I met when he was seventeen years old, received a scholarship from the Berklee College of Music Summer 5-Week Program while at the detention center. His name is Matt, and he is now in his thirties and doing extremely well. Matt started a band that has been quite successful and is very active. On my birthday in 2014, Matt emailed me out of blue. "Hey, I don't know if you remember me. About ten years ago, you taught me a little piano and guitar. Anyway, I just want to thank you for doing what you do. I wouldn't be the musician I am today if it weren't for that program (Genuine Voices)."

I am so humbled to know our program contributed to Matt's accomplishment as a musician. All you need is one person to believe in another, and for Matt, it was this small investment of time and encouragement that changed the course of his life completely. I'm so proud of you and love you, Matt!

Another boy we taught in the detention program was an excellent drummer. All of my volunteer teachers raved about his drumming skills and outgoing personality. He performed with me at some concerts and fundraisers after his release as well as playing with other musicians I knew. He accompanied me to one of my speaking engagements at a college, and I split my payment with him. He was also featured with me on Japanese TV. He told me Genuine Voices motivated him, not just musically, but in life, to be the best he could be. He went on to start his own T-shirt company. I am so proud of him.

There are many success stories like the ones above, but overall, it was not easy, as you can imagine. We were teaching a difficult segment of our society. These were children who mostly grew up in poverty, with minimal parenting and community support, little guidance, no real role models, limited resources, and most importantly, little expression of love.

Over the twelve years I taught in the program, the one thing I truly believe is that the majority of these kids are good at heart. Unfortunately, the environment they grew up in was so rough, they needed to become tough themselves to survive and to fit in. From my own experience, I know what it's like to feel like you have to be someone you're not, simply because you see no way out. Some kids I met harbored anger that was boiling under their skin, yet they couldn't express it. In many ways, it reminded me of my childhood.

I remember teaching piano to one boy whose hands began to shake. When I asked if he was okay, he opened up, tearfully sharing that when he was only five years old, his father was shot to death in front of his own eyes. As a result, he became the man of the house at a young age and a big brother/father figure to his little sister. One day his sister was being beaten up by neighbors, and in her defense, he punched one of her assailants and broke a boy's rib. He was unfairly charged with assault and was forced to serve time in a detention center. He confided in me that it cost him his childhood, that life was unfair, and he wasn't sure how to continue. I wrote him a special song, recorded it, and gifted it to him. His counselor later told me he loved my song and was listening to it every night. With the care he received not only from me but also from our volunteer music teachers, he was doing well after his release.

I always told the volunteer teachers that music is a tool to bring souls closer by building self-esteem and trust. Teaching music can nurture students in the detention program to open up, because you may be the only one a student may trust, and the music was what made that possible a lot of times. I have hired truly amazing volunteers and interns who were selfless and genuinely caring. Because of the mission and work, we were able to provide the gift of music lessons within our community, especially to the most vulnerable of the population. Genuine Voices' mission truly attracted pure souls who wanted to help others. I am so grateful and cannot thank all the people who came into my life and helped my vision, students, and our community.

BLOODS AND CRIPS

The Boston probation officer, who had told me I didn't know anything about gangs in America and how they operate, was right. But I was about to learn firsthand. My baptism came when I began teaching full time at a detention center. I was the first full-time music teacher ever in the Massachusetts detention center system. The facility I taught in was considered to have the worst offenders in the state, where some teens continued straight to adult correctional institutions for the crimes they committed. I always felt there were reasons for this violent behavior, and usually, reading a teen's profile helped explain their situation.

The majority of these kids' parents were in jail or addicted to drugs. Some kids yoyoed between the DYS (Department of Youth Services) and DCF (Department of Children and Families) for most of their teen years. DYS is for the kids who committed crimes; DCF is for kids whose parents had problems and lost custody of their kids. It's easy to see how fragile these youth are. Some were raised by foster parents who didn't do a good job and were in it just to collect checks from the system. These kids needed a sense of belonging, and my theory in observing these teens was that the majority skipped their innocent years, having to grow up on their own at a young age. I sensed sadness, loneliness, and hopelessness in these young people, at a time when their future was in front of them.

This is only my personal opinion, but I think belonging to the gang provided that sense of family and loyalty to those who never received the love and sense of belonging growing up. I saw students in gangs that were as close as family. A gang provided a brotherhood; they had each other's back, very much like a family. If someone hurt one of the members, the gang would retaliate against that person. Also, some may have purposefully returned to the detention facility due to lack of food and guidance, but in the detention center, they would get three meals, healthcare, education, counseling, and familiar friends. One time I was talking to one boy, who was probably sixteen or seventeen years old, and asked what his dream was. He looked into my eyes and said, "I don't have a dream, because as soon as I am out, I know I will be killed." So, there was no point for this young boy to dream.

The gangs I came to know through the detention system in Massachusetts were the Blood gang and the Crips gang. I had no idea how much gang blood was infused in the lives of these young people. The mentality of both the Blood and Crips gang originated in California, but the concept spread across the country, including the Boston area. There are specific areas where the majority of these gangs live. The majority of the Blood gang in the Boston area speak Spanish, a language I was not familiar with. I became motivated to learn Spanish because I wanted to understand and develop a good rapport with my students. It also helped to be able to interpret the underlining verbiage the kids thought was just between them. For this reason, I started to learn Spanish on my own.

The Blood gang always wore the color red, whereas the Crips wore blue. I remember one time I was in a classroom dominated by Blood gang members, and I highlighted students' names who completed a piano assignment in blue. One of the students asked me why I was using the color blue in the classroom. "You know what we are," he said.

I didn't take it as a threat and simply replied: "Because that was the highlighter that I had." They respected my answer and there was no incident. But it was an interesting learning experience about how gangs think. I still don't truly understand all that is involved, but now have an inkling into the culture and code.

A lot of people asked if I was scared of teaching gang members in a detention center, but truthfully, I never was. Prison is one of the places in America that has 100 percent gun control. The kids, by and large, really enjoyed music and were receptive to me teaching them. I became popular, especially when I was a full-time teacher and with them on almost a daily basis. Due to confidentiality, I cannot write about specific incidents, but some drama that happened at work did take its toll physically and emotionally. My husband (the first) suggested I quit, but I tried to tough it out for the students. When my grandmother passed away, I went back to Japan and vomited some blood. It all became too much, and I decided to submit my resignation letter for the full-time position.

All in all, I honestly learned so much immersing myself with these students. From playing basketball with them during my lunch break to watching them embrace music, it was an amazing experience to see the transformation from gang member to individual. To me, they were all just lost souls who needed some sense of belonging. Except for a few kids who gave me absolute hell, I enjoyed getting to know each one of them, because I empathized with their pain and I think they saw me as a kindred spirit. Or, I may say they smelled my adversity and were able to relate to it.

I remember talking to a young man who was an amazing rapper but had found himself at the detention center after selling drugs off and on since the age of thirteen. As I spoke, he would not make eye contact, and I wasn't sure I was getting through. I shared some of the adversities I went through in Japan, and all of a sudden, his eyes opened wide and he said, "So you went through hell like me."

I looked at him, finally eye to eye, and told him, "Yes, that is why I want to help you, and I know I can help you." Later on, he participated in some fundraisers and did an amazing job performing. He had a great way of expressing his struggles through rap music. I was so proud of him.

In 2020, I ran into this young man, who is now in his twenties, in downtown Boston. He screamed my name, as I did the same, and we hugged and talked. Most importantly, he had a huge smile on his face, and he now is doing well in life.

FROM CRIMINAL TO ROCK STAR

When you think of criminals, a majority of us think they're bad guys. We are biased that criminals are bad people. In some cases, I believe that to be very true, but in some cases I have seen, not so much. When I meet boys who are so misguided by a lack of parenting, little guidance, and no one there to rescue them, I think at some level it is society's responsibility to provide reform. But many do not think this way. Programs cost money, and many people are not willing to see their tax dollars spent on programs, which is just my humble opinion. When I was running Genuine Voices, I had one message to our volunteers: "You are the one who can determine whether they stay a criminal or become a rock star in the future, by your expectations. Especially if, as teachers and mentors, you believe these young people will never learn or reform, then they will become exactly what you expect. But if you see the potential and foster the idea that they are the future, that you believe in them by letting them know you care and provide your support, they will thrive."

I believe the biggest challenge educators face in teaching is to do so without bias. As educators, it is we who are in charge of showing children their potential. If you treat juvenile delinquents like they are Harvard University students and teach them at the highest level, they will learn. Conversely, and what I think happens much too often, these students are considered lost and it is assumed they will never learn. As a result, the student also believes they have no potential and lives up to that expectation.

I believe this concept also applies to parents. If parents believe their children are not that smart and don't motivate them to be their best, then they will likely end up with children who meet that expectation. However, parents who encourage their children to reach high and become resources to help them achieve their goals will likely see their offspring achieve an incredible level of success. Let your children know they are the best and you love them and believe in them every single day. I am sure they will thrive to their full potential.

If your students are not doing well, I recommend talking to their teachers to see how the educators' brains are wired. Most educators are top-notch and want your child to succeed, but some are biased based on many factors, including social status and race. My point is simply that if you want your students to grow to their full potential, you need to ensure both home and school foster an environment that allows them to aspire to their very best.

I remember telling our students in the detention program how good they are and how much they have accomplished in music. They always had these priceless smiles on their faces. In the end, they all seemed to be proud of receiving praise, and who doesn't love getting praised on their effort on this earth anyway?

AS A LEADER

As a president and founder of a small yet mighty organization, I had several opportunities to meet leaders and researchers from around the world. On one such occasion, I was invited to be on a panel as part of a research project with some Australian professors at the IASPM (The International Association for the Study of Popular Music) Conference in Rome, Italy. I learned how research, public speaking, and book publication play such an important role in larger funding, especially from government and other grant subsidies. I was also asked and honored to contribute my experiences to a book called *Youth, Music and Creative Cultures: Playing for Life* by Geraldine Bloustien and Margaret Peters. Please check the book out online or request it at a local library. Thank you, Gerry and Margaret, for this amazing opportunity to collaborate with you on a topic so dear to my heart.

As the leader of Genuine Voices, I wore a great many hats, meaning I served in several roles. Beyond president and founder, I contributed to marketing, hiring (HR), grant writing (often a full-time job in itself), event planning (i.e. fundraising), donor appreciation, cultivating a rapport with donors and supported foundations, accounting (thank you, Bo, for your generous service for twelve years), filing various paperwork, program management, creating community connections, detention program contact, volunteer oversight, website and social media management, branding, and public relations. You name it, I did it all.

When writing grant applications and doing research, I also learned a new term: tangible, measurable outcome. An example of a tangible, measurable outcome is when you teach a simple piano song or hip-hop production and youth can hear the outcome, which is tangible and measurable (i.e. you can hear the song). This concept promotes self-esteem, self-confidence, and a sense of ownership, which can lead to building resilience and is important when lowering recidivism. I have applied this method in parenting in a bold way. In 2018, my children and I flew to New Mexico. I let my son pick out an inexpensive vacant plot of land so he could learn how to invest in real estate with his earnings from his modeling job, which he has been doing since he was three years old (now he is almost ten). But there was more to it than that. I wanted him to also feel that sense of ownership that comes with owning a small piece of earth—an extreme example of a tangible, measurable outcome—which I hope will contribute to his self-confidence and build his resilience for whenever he may face adversity in his life.

You never know how gaining new knowledge, such as starting and running a nonprofit, can potentially help not only your future but that of the next generation. As I gain more knowledge in finance and investment, sometimes I share the concept with some of the youths we taught whom I am still in touch with. In the end, I would never have learned about tangible, measurable outcomes without Genuine Voices.

People have varying opinions on what makes a good leader. I tried to be the best leader I could. Something I feel that worked for me was saying a simple thank-you and giving your staff 100 percent trust and support. Easier said than done, especially as a leader. In some cases, you feel a need for control, and that might lead to micromanagement, which the majority of people hate. Giving 100 percent of your trust and support unleashes the potential of your staff and their creativity. I have had countless conversations with our staff on how much they felt trusted and appreciated by me, and truthfully we had some long-term volunteer staff who volunteered throughout their four years of college because they felt trusted and worthy of doing that amount of work. I particularly want to thank Hannah and Oliver, both at the time music therapy majors, for their dedication to change lives in the detention programs through Genuine Voices.

As a leader, simple appreciation goes a long way. When you lead without thanking those who help, people quickly lose their motivation to work hard. This is especially true with volunteers, who receive no payment for their service. Without acknowledgment of their efforts, you may find they do not sustain their effort for long. On the other hand, a thank-you costs nothing, yet makes people feel their contributions were appreciated and worthwhile. For a volunteer, there is no better feeling, and as a leader, there is such satisfaction in knowing your workers feel good about their contribution. Such a powerful tool at such little cost.

One issue I struggled with as a leader was conflict management and resolution. Due to my trauma, I became nervous when people around me were in conflict, and especially when I encountered conflict with older men with authority. I would tense up and become unable to communicate well. I explained my problem when attending the Institute for Nonprofit Management and Leadership Core Certificate Program at Boston University School of Management (from October 2, 2012, to May 1, 2013), and one of my classmates said something I consider brilliant. She said, "Juri, don't think or treat conflict as an issue or problem. If you need to confront someone, just think it as a conversation and see the other side of the conversation." That advice helped me a lot. Another teacher told me when addressing a conflict with someone you have a close relationship with, inform your coworker that you have to wear a leader hat for the balance of the discussion, but after that, you are friends. Both pieces of advice helped me.

The best leaders have an insightful and powerful vision and recognize their limitations. It is important to know yourself as a leader, and bravely understand your weaknesses and use your team to cover areas you don't excel in. This means being able to admit that weakness and ask for help. People have various skills, and part of being a good leader is recognizing those skills in other people and leveraging them to cover your deficiencies for the good of the team. Doing so is a pathway to successfully grow your organization and develop a great rapport. But it means being brutally honest with yourself and sharing that honesty with your team. By and large, humble people are always willing to help you, but you must earn their respect, and a good measure of that comes from being strong enough to admit your weaknesses. For instance, one of my weaknesses is writing English. My native language is Japanese, so for me, grant writing was very difficult. I recognized my deficiency in writing English and asked one of the board members, who had written numerous grants, to supervise our interns who were working on the grant drafts. It worked out beautifully.

I also think a big part of being a good leader is being kind and fostering the growth of your team. Equally important is formally recognizing their accomplishments and letting them know personally how proud you are of their work.

Finally, as a leader, I believe it's important to set a good example by staying healthy, eating healthy foods, being a positive force, and conveying an energetic vibe that your team will feed off of. I have learned a lot as a leader and hope I made a positive influence and difference for the twelve years I held a leadership role.

REALIZING AN IDEA

After twelve years of running a nonprofit organization, I learned a lot, but one of the more important things was that if you have an idea, there are many ways to realize it. Today, between the internet and applications like YouTube, there are many information sources available that offer help. But do not be afraid to ask questions to those people already doing what you desire to do. I have found that most people are willing to help if you approach them humbly and appreciably. And try not to forget to say thank-you, two of the most valuable words you can ever share. A thank-you can get you beyond your intentions and further than you might imagine. I also came to realize that most people appreciate straightforward questions, such as how did you get from point A to point B? How did you do that? Is there a secret? How much does it cost? What kind of resources did you use? Etc.

People don't want you to waste their time, but I found that people like to be asked and are mostly willing to help. I have asked millions of questions to get to where I am, and while some questions may have annoyed a few people along the way, it is exactly how I received many of my answers. If you don't ask, you won't get the answer. Don't be afraid. I often notice some people are afraid to ask favors because they don't want to get rejected. I understand *no one* likes rejection, yet I always tell people you only have two answers, YES or NO, so if the chances are 50/50, why not ask?

One time I was at the car wash and noticed a gentleman there who looked like the owner. I started an informal conversation with him, and after verifying that he was the owner, I asked him, "How did you start your car wash business?" He explained everything to me, including attaining a permit from the town and how much various pieces of equipment cost. He even told me about a $10,000 door he just installed. I felt certain if I had the capital and asked him to be my mentor, he would have said yes. After explaining his business to me in detail, he offered me an ultra-shine car wash package, which was the most expensive option—

FREE OF CHARGE. I not only got a business lesson from him but also got my car super washed and waxed for free!

In Japanese, there is a saying: *Yuugen jikkou* (有言実行), meaning, "You talk about your idea and you act on it." The concept is to follow through on what you say you will do. It's not always easy, which is why many people don't follow through. But my philosophy is *Hatsuan suikou* （発案遂行), which is my made-up Japanese phrase meaning, "When you get an idea, execute it."

Speaking too much about your ideas can be counterproductive because some people may take a negative view and you may get discouraged. They may not see your vision or have the same perspective you do. You could have a truly great idea that someone without context or perspective could think was useless. Yet to those who could benefit, it may be life-changing. My philosophy is to execute on ideas rather than ask for opinions. If you're going to consult, ask those who have done what you want to do and can contribute to getting your idea realized. Time is often limited, so use your intuition to guide you. Most times you won't go wrong.

I've had numerous ideas, especially while I was running Genuine Voices. Fortunately, I worked with a great team of people who were fast thinkers, and we were able to implement and execute many creative project notions.

One successful project I am proud of likely never would have happened if I had asked around versus jumping to execution mode. It was a collaboration between Princeton University student Erica, who was Genuine Voices' summer intern, and her friend, who was donating original songs to children in hospitals and local nonprofit Urbanity Dance. We asked our students in one detention center to donate a song to a pediatric cancer patient we found through GoFundMe (a fundraising website). One of the boys we asked for in this program was considered one of the most dangerous juvenile offenders in the state of Massachusetts. He was incarcerated at a very young age and spent most of his teenage life in a detention center.

It was a challenge for the students to write and rap some positive lyrics on the production because many of them were heavily influenced by "gangsta rap," which can contain many swear words and lyrics condoning killing, having sex, money, and the like. It was always a struggle between the teens and our staff, as a song to a pediatric cancer patient can't contain that content. Surprisingly, the student I mentioned wrote a most compassionate song that touched us in a way we could not believe. No one had ever seen that side of him, and it was a total shock to many, especially the staff at the detention center.

We reached out to Urbanity Dance to inquire if their dancers could choreograph the music. At our fundraiser, the student was able to get a community pass and attended the venue escorted by the director and supervisor from the detention center. He shared a beautiful testimony to about a hundred people, and when his song was played, three beautiful dancers performed a moving dance to his composition. His eyes sparkled, and he seemed mesmerized by these dancers dancing to his composition. We were so proud of him and gratified that we were able to provide this opportunity.

It was a prime example of an idea that, if discussed, might never have happened. A hardened detention center student writing music for a pediatric cancer patient, which a dance company then choreographs, seems preposterous in theory, but the results spoke for themselves. Some of life's greatest rewards come from executing and not overthinking.

CHAPTER 5

Black and White

THE FIRST TIME I HEARD THE ACRONYM PTSD WAS IN 1999, from a counselor at my college. She told me PTSD means post-traumatic stress disorder, and after learning about it, my own life began to make more sense. I could explain why every time something that reminded me of the past happened, I couldn't sleep or eat and often lost my motivation for days. Before learning about PTSD, I was so confused about why I felt depressed and would cry for long periods. I never gave counseling a chance. A part of it could be that in Japan, the concept of counseling shows one's weakness and is an embarrassment. When I finally gave counseling a shot, the few counselors I met, in my opinion, all appeared to care nothing about my struggle and seemed they were there to just get paid. They seemed to know nothing about adversity and just watched the clock tick.

In 2003, when I was working part time at Starbucks, my boss yelled at me and it triggered something within me so bad that I could not eat or sleep for almost a week. I somehow found the courage to discuss the incident and my reaction with my boss. He recommended I seek professional help and informed me that counseling sessions were part of my employee benefits. He said I could try the first three counseling sessions free of charge.

I hated the idea of attending counseling, recalling my past experiences. I decided to go to one session, probably because it would be paid for and would allow me to say I tried. I honestly had no intention of attending more than one. But the counselor I met at that time turned out to be truly amazing and helped me. I think she sensed my lack of interest and somehow read my emotional state. I remember as I was walking out from her room with the intention of not coming back, she stood at the door and said, "Juri, I became a counselor not only because I read a lot of books, but also because I, too, am a victim of sexual abuse, just like you." After she shared that confidence, I decided to give her a shot. Well, she won my trust, and this thing called "counseling" ended up being a weekly event for six years until she moved to a different state.

During one of our first sessions, she explained to me how she billed insurance to help me understand PTSD. She said if I was mentally ill, she would use a specific code and insurance would cover the cost of thirty-two sessions for the year. But PTSD is a switch of chemicals in the brain and is considered a biological condition. Therefore, it requires a different code and would entitle me to thirty-three sessions a year. I might be incorrect regarding the exact number of sessions, but the point she made was that I wouldn't be ashamed to see a doctor for any other biological illness, like cancer. Why, then, should I hesitate to get help for this biological condition to get myself better? It was such an eye-opening conversation, and it sure made me feel better to accept the concept of counseling.

I learned so much from her. But I am not going to lie—it was one of the most difficult things I have ever done in my life. It helped through episodes of forcing myself to vomit, something she told me was not unusual for clients with PTSD. This and other incidents of inflicting pain or replaying the trauma via physical pain are a means to help the inflicted person feel grounded.

In 2004, I vividly remember when Hollywood actor Tim Robbins won an Academy Award as Best Supporting Actor for the film *Mystic River*, playing the role of Dave Boyle, a victim of childhood sexual abuse. During Robbins's acceptance speech, he said, "Going to counseling is one of the strongest things you can do." His words inspired me and gave me the courage to continue my counseling because, at that time, I still harbored doubt about the benefits of seeking treatment.

After my lovely counselor, Amanda (thank you very much, Amanda), moved away and I wasn't sure what my next steps should be, two of my friends, who were also victims of domestic violence and sexual abuse, recommended I consider doing an EMDR (eye movement desensitization and reprocessing). It had worked miraculously for them and their PTSD. Coincidently, an EMDR-certified counselor shared an office with a counselor I knew from prior sessions, and I signed up with her to take sessions. During one of our first sessions, she showed me a plastic model of the brain and told me that trauma is stored in the primitive part of the brain, the limbic system. When something triggers that part of the brain, it fires up and shuts down the cognitive part of the brain. In doing so, it produces behavior where people can't speak, freeze up, can't eat, etc. Or, it invokes a fight-or-flight response.

I am hardly an expert, but I recall my counselor telling me the goal of EMDR is to bring the trauma stored in the primitive part of the brain to the cognitive part, so it can be processed in a way the client understands and can rationalize. She told me to think of the worst thing that happened to me while administering the right-to-left stimulation. After five minutes, she asked me to explain what I saw, conveying it as though I were watching a movie. It is interesting how bringing the trauma to the cognitive part of the brain and talking through it helps the mind settle and process it.

After a few EMDR treatments, I felt much better. There is a wealth of information on EMDR on the internet if you wish to learn more. If you are suffering from PTSD, I highly recommend finding a local certified therapist and exploring EMDR as a treatment option. I thought the treatments helped me a lot.

EMDR is just one means to combat PTSD. There are many other treatments, and what works for one may not work for another. If you have PTSD, you have my full support. Know there is a way to cope and deal with it. Trust me, you are not alone, and I tried many different methods. Just be open-minded and let yourself heal.

THYROID DISEASE AND CHAKRA

I mentioned earlier that when I was twenty years old, I was diagnosed with the hyperthyroid disease. Some years later, after my son was born in 2012, I was diagnosed with a hypothyroid disease, the opposite of what I had when I was in Japan.

With my TSH (thyroid-stimulating hormone) test value being four times higher than normal levels (my TSH was around sixteen), my doctor prescribed medication and informed me I would need medication to regulate my thyroid for the rest of my life. She warned me I would be unlikely to conceive and I might lose my hair, in addition to some other unpleasant side effects. I wasn't ready to accept this diagnosis and was less ready to accept the treatment. I was no longer a naïve Japanese girl. I had lived in America for almost fourteen years at the time of this diagnosis and knew there were other options, and that I have my own choices and rights.

Instead of following my doctor's direction, I investigated alternative ways to address this condition (not sickness or disease, the key is to use the word "condition"). A friend introduced me to someone who experienced similar circumstances and was acquainted with NRT (nutrition response testing). This was a diet-based treatment and I jumped in, changing my diet entirely.

Fourteen months later, my TSH value returned to a normal level. I had cured my thyroid issue without taking a single pill and by simply altering what I ate. No sugar, no caffeine, no artificial flavors, using sea salt, eating alkaline food, and of course, organic food was my mainstay. The best part of the treatment was that I was able to get pregnant and deliver a healthy and gorgeous baby girl, Jayla, in 2016. All without taking medication and dealing with any dangerous side effects. Many people have asked me about this process. I think most people, when diagnosed with a thyroid condition and when a Western doctor says they need to take medicine for the rest of their life, follow the doctor's order out of fear. But in Eastern medicine or a different perspective, it might not be true, and you just have to listen to your instinct. I was talking to my NRT practitioner about my awful surgery in Japan, and she said, "I wish I met you then. You didn't have to do the surgery." I believe she is right, as she guided me to cure the condition without medication.

In 2015, I became a Reiki practitioner. In Reiki class, there is a lot of discussion about chakra. I did some research on the throat chakra and found that it correlates to depression, early issues of abandonment and separation, difficulty with relationships, and an increased risk of infectious disease (i.e. cancer, AIDS, etc.). I found that my thyroid problems may have been related to my trauma, and of course eating "toxic" food. This mind/body combination could have contributed to the imbalance that created my thyroid condition. Of course, this is subjective, but it provides a rational explanation for my thyroid disease.

A traumatic experience can damage you in many aspects. This includes mentally—depression, low self-esteem (I suffer from low self-esteem to this day; however, so many of my friends have told me I am beautiful inside and out), lack of trust, etc.—and physically (in my case, thyroid disease). I didn't know how much my body was suffering from this trauma. However, I considered myself strong and able to conquer any adversity. I never realized how much my mind and body were crying out for help.

ANGEL NUMBER 11 AND MY VIEW ON SEXUALITY

This might be the most vulnerable thing I share in this book. One day, a friend told me about "Angel Number 11." Some people believe Angel Number 11 represents inspiration and enlightenment (you can search it on Google if you're curious and want to learn more). It is based on the promise that your angels want you to act on the things that make you happy and fulfilled and provide a sense of purpose in your life. The message is to connect with your higher self, come to know your soul mission, and live your life's purpose. It is also a call to be an inspiration and bring light to others.

I have seen reference to number eleven many times, such as when I look at a clock depicting 11:11, or a house or building address. For me, the number eleven represents both good and bad. It makes me consider that eleven is the number of men I slept with during the four months in between my first marriage until I met my second husband and became pregnant with my first son. I believe this is extremely important to share; however, it takes all my courage, for it is the time in my life that I take no pride in.

During my first marriage, the demons of my trauma, at the

hands of my father, found me. I was depressed and in a dark place and treated my husband at the time (my first husband) horribly. I neglected him, cheated on him, and finally left him. (Karma caught me in 2019 when I became a single mother.) My first husband was, and still is, such an angel, given that I hurt him so badly. He has forgiven me. I know I cannot blame everything on my trauma, but unfortunately, what happened, happened, and destroyed a beautiful relationship. It led to another victim that I feel could have been prevented, had I educated myself earlier about PTSD.

There is a book titled *Waking the Tiger: Healing Trauma* by Dr. Peter A. Levine. I highly recommend the book, as it explains well what happened to me. The book was a recommendation from a friend, and for me was such a game-changer. One of the key passages I remember was that lots of trauma victims reorchestrate their trauma. That is exactly how I acted out with my first husband, recreating a huge dramatic situation and leaving. That and sleeping around, hoping to prove sex was meant to be something special, not a violation. Looking back now, it makes little sense and explains why during my teenage years through my early twenties, my relationships never lasted more than eight months or so.

I believe the reaction is to look for corrective experience and gain back control that you lost, especially when it comes to sex. To me, sex is some kind of chore; there is nothing sacred about it and my mind will wander off to completely different things while having sex. I think it is because I was so afraid during my sexual abuse, yet remember some sensation of arousal at such a young age. When I get scared, I have this strange urge to have sex, but not necessarily satisfy my sexual needs. Rather, I want to gain power over my fear and take control of having sex, so that not getting violated somehow makes me feel empowered.

Sadly, for me, talking about sex conjures memories of the most unfortunate part of my life. But I know it is important to share, because for those who experience sexual abuse, not only is their purity or faith in humanity most impacted, so, too, is their heart. Once shattered, a heart is often beyond repair, and it becomes impossible for some people to open again. It is truly sad, and I would not wish this on anyone.

I wish I had read Peter Levine's book earlier in my life and gained a better understanding of why I was continuously orchestrating unnecessary drama. Amid the storm, you have no idea of the impact abuse can have on your life and the lives of those around you. You live in a distorted view draped in darkness, and sometimes your mind controls your actions no matter how hard you resist, without any logical explanation.

As I have grown older and, perhaps, a little wiser, I have come to understand my struggle toward life better. In doing so, I see more of the number eleven, which has inspired me to share my life and my gift from adversity.

Recently, I met a wonderful integration coach, Otto, who teaches this mantra at the start of his transformative breathwork class: "I am the love that I seek." This mantra resonated with me deeply. After the sexual abuse, I was always seeking the healthy love that I did not receive from my father. This formed the foundation of my sexual addiction, in which I was continually seeking "true love" as a test to see if anyone could love me. But after learning this powerful mantra, I realized I was seeking love from a source that could never bring me fulfillment. This concept completely opened my eyes and I became able to truly understand why I had been destroying myself by sleeping with random men.

I had been wrong about where I could find love. I had never thought to look inward to find that I am the love and light I had been seeking all alone. Therefore, I had to realize I need to treat myself gently and cherish my life because *I am the love that I seek.* Thank you, Otto, for sharing your wisdom.

I deeply hope that sharing my personal story can touch those out there struggling with trauma and help them realize, much faster than me, that they have a condition requiring professional help. I hope by reading my story they can sidestep the mistakes I made. I hope victims will see value, both in themselves and in their lives, and know with certainty what happened was NOT YOUR FAULT! I hold optimism that those reading this book will take a second look at themselves and see the beauty and strength that flourishes within. That they realize if they are reading this book, they still have more to accomplish on this earth. I truly believe my adversity has helped me grow more beautifully, internally and externally. Now, I feel I am able to move forward in a completely different light that I can illuminate others with.

ER BILL AND SUICIDE PREVENTION HOTLINE

At one point, the health insurance I carried was MassHealth. Its cost was determined by the income of an individual. During a summer job, a situation arose with my boss, and he began yelling at me over the phone. His outburst triggered a serious panic attack where I was crying and hyperventilating. I asked my ex-husband (the second) to take me to the emergency room of my local hospital, without knowing any of the financial consequences. When I arrived at the emergency room, the ER doctor took my vitals. A nurse withdrew blood, and after four hours, I left with a bruise from where blood had been drawn.

A week later I received an invoice from the hospital, for just under $4,000. That averages about $1,000 per hour of stay and is on par with some of the most expensive hotels in the world. I called MassHealth and was informed that their records showed my income three times higher than actual. Nonetheless, they informed me my coverage carried a $13,000 deductible, therefore I was responsible for the entire hospital bill. I was devastated.

Even today I carry credit card debt from that hospital visit. It was a sobering experience, and I told myself I would *not* pay $4,000 for another a panic attack! Every time I see my credit card statement and the balance from that medical bill, my blood pressure rises, and I get a little angry about that ER visit. Ironically, ever since then, my panic attacks have ceased significantly.

Another interesting thing that happened to me to help stop my suicidal thoughts was seeing a wonderful acupuncturist. I mentioned to her that I suffered from suicidal thoughts due to PTSD. Her approach was to have me sign a contract, which stated when suicidal thoughts occurred, I would reach out to three people (she let me write their names and phone numbers) or contact her. She told me the contract was between her and me, and additionally provided me the number of the suicide prevention hotline.

One day, a difficult event I can't recall triggered something in me and I was struggling to see myself continue another day. I called the hotline number she gave me, which was saved on my phone. I recall the worker who picked up the phone sounded super happy. He used the highest-pitched, most flamboyant tones imaginable, saying, "Oh my God, honey, I am so sorry. It will be okay . . . Oh no, darling . . . We are here for you 24/7! You can call us back anytime . . . Honey, it is going to be okay!"

His voice and personality cheered me up so much and stopped my suicidal thoughts after our joyful conversation. I never found out who was on the phone when I called, but I send a huge thank-you. You saved me that night.

PERSPECTIVE

One of the things I always found difficult before I started my counseling sessions was confrontation, especially with a man, as I mentioned earlier. If I had a different opinion than a man, I always felt something awful would happen if I spoke out, because that had been the scene growing up. No matter how nice the man was, I would become scared and too tongue-tied to share my mind. Over the years, I have gotten better at it, but it has been a long road to be able to advocate for myself.

One day, when I was teaching music for the detention program for Genuine Voices, I witnessed one boy being rude to another. Because of the nature of the detention program and the emotional issues the kids carry, it can trigger volatile situations, and at first, I was afraid to say anything. It took all my courage to say he was rude, should apologize, and never to do it again, and the boy followed my direction.

When I told my counselor about the episode, she did not take it lightly. I remember she got off from her comfortable chair and cheered for me, jumping up and down and saying she was proud. I didn't realize it was such a big deal until she kindly brought it to my attention. This may appear a small achievement, but most people don't understand how emotionally draining an experience like this can be. My counselor told me this kind of experience is called a "corrective experience." What this means is that each time I stand up for myself, I am helping correct the years of conditioning, where, if I spoke my mind, I'd be punished for it.

Little by little, I began to see positive things happening to me. With more corrective experiences like that, I became more comfortable with confrontation or giving my opinion, without getting emotional or succumbing to panic attacks. Well, let's say I at least overcame the fear of getting beaten up because of having a different opinion than others. For me, this was a huge victory, that I could now feel okay and safe to share my opinion.

Confrontation was not the only area I've had to work through via counseling. Some of my deepest fears are from the physical and sexual abuse I endured in my formative years. To deal with some of my issues associated with PTSD, my counselor encouraged me to think about black paper and white paper. She told me the color of white is much brighter when the color of black is right next to it. I didn't get the metaphor she was trying to explain at that time, but now, years later, after having two beautiful children, it has become clear. If I had never endured the dark days and pain, I might have been more inclined to take the love of my children for granted. Now, each day, I am so grateful to have two beautiful children, Jaden and Jayla, and amazing friends around me. Whenever my children say, "Mama, I love you, おかあさんだいすき (Okaasan daisuki, "I love you, Mom" in Japanese)," it just melts my heart. But again, if I didn't know how special these small gestures and words are, I may not deeply appreciate it and give them the best and warmest hugs in return. I especially appreciate this because I know there is another sordid existence one can experience that is so overwhelming it is a struggle just to survive.

I am eternally grateful my suicide attempts never came to fruition and that I was able to conceive children, and hopefully will see grandchildren in the future. Yes, it absolutely sucked, no better way to say it, but again, white is so much brighter when next to black. Therefore, you must trust me when I say every negative experience or piece of adversity that finds you is finite and will have an end. Beyond that, I know from firsthand experience it will only brighten your true happiness when it finds you. You may even have the key and courage to change that perspective right now. So please, never give up. I send you a virtual hug and a tremendous amount of unconditional love and support to survive another day from any adversity you may be facing.

CHAPTER 6

Hope and the Meaning of Happiness

AS I'VE MENTIONED, I HAVE AMAZING FRIENDS— friends from Japan, friends I met after arriving in America. All these extraordinary people have truly helped me conquer my many challenges and adversities. Supportive friends who told me I was beautiful and talented when I didn't feel that way at all, and friends who completely believed in me and bolstered me with their confidence and faith. But it did not start that way. I think that applies to everyone; there is a rite of passage an individual must live through before they find their way in the world. I am the type of person who does things quickly and, hopefully, efficiently. I am extremely motivated to live and pass my motivation to others. Some people do not appreciate these traits. Some find me pushy and intimidating, not seeing my help as assistance, but as an annoyance. Some simply see me as a threat. But the people I call my friends today and those I keep close are 100 percent by my choice. And I choose to surround myself with great people carefully. My secret or technique? I choose friends who are accomplished and way more inspirational than me. I choose friends who have the drive and motivation to penetrate the world with their love and kindness.

Yes, friends are made and kept completely by your choice. So, if you're not comfortable with the friends you have, perhaps it's time to evaluate that friendship. With so little time to spare in our lives, we want to ensure we spend it in the best way possible, with the people who make us feel loved and inspired. Today never comes back, so be smart and be alert about who you are opening your life to. There are also various levels of friendships and relationships you can make. At the end of the day, those are all your responsibility. You must decide how much you let each in. I've certainly made mistakes about "friends" that I thought were truly my friends, and I let them in only to be betrayed, used, or dismissed. I'm sure we all experience this, but more reason to consider your friendships seriously. Making a conscious choice about whom you entrust as a friend and surround yourself with is important. Because we all need good friends to help us survive this crazy life every day.

Probably the most important thing I needed to learn about friendship was to reach out to friends when in need. I never was good at reaching out, especially when I was depressed or suffering from PTSD. It took the birth of my son, when I needed help, to reach out to my friends. Of course, they were all there for me. My son taught me a huge life lesson, which is to reach out. I guess I shouldn't have been surprised to learn that most of the time, people are happy to help you. It works the same with me, as I'm always happy to help others. But sometimes it requires overcoming conditioning from your childhood or whatever the reasons may be for not feeling comfortable asking help from friends. If that's you, please know most of us can feel amazing when someone reaches out and can help.

The one thing I may not have emphasized about friendship, but is paramount to any good friendship, is that friendships are two-way streets. Right now, all my friends are incredible human beings and I can confidently say would do nearly anything for me. But the flip side of that is that they know, without a doubt, that I'm there for them and would do anything for them. It was never easy for me to trust anyone, and it is still a challenge. But you can't learn to swim if you never get in the water; you never know until you try.

It is only natural for trauma survivors to have issues dealing with trust and making friends. Given where they have come from, I can completely understand and deeply empathize with their struggle. It sometimes helps to consider that your abuser may have themselves been abused and had no real friends. It is in your control to make friends and reach out to others, asking, "Do you wanna be my friend?" My son and daughter are super awesome in this way. We go to the playground, basketball court, every-where together, and within five minutes they are playing with everyone around them.

I admire the lack of inhibition in them so deeply. Seeing them make friends so easily is something I am proud of. All I want in the future for both of my children is to have no fear of humans. I never want my children to experience the unnecessary fear I ex-perienced. Fortunately for me, I am proud to say, I overcame my fear, and seeing my son and daughter enjoy a peaceful life, sur-rounded by friends, makes me even happier. To see the love and affection that greets my children when they meet their friends warms my heart. Friendship, especially life-lasting ones, can be magnificently important and beautiful.

A SMILE AFTER TWO MISCARRIAGES

I am currently a single mother of two beautiful children (I divorced my second husband of ten years on September 25, 2019): a very athletic, handsome son, Jaden (jadenonwuakor.com), who was born on October 31, 2010, and my gorgeous daughter, Jayla, who was born on June 1, 2016. They make me proud and give me a solid reason to live every day.

I had two miscarriages after my son was born. My first miscarriage was in 2014. My baby had a low heartbeat at the first ultrasound, but it stopped at nine weeks and three days. I was so devastated . . . it was the worst feeling in the world. Something dies inside of you. I cried nonstop when the doctor informed me my baby's heartbeat had stopped. I don't believe I could put into words the devastation of losing a baby.

I didn't realize until I shared my experience that there are far too many women who have experienced a miscarriage. It certainly made me take notice of how precious life is. It is a gift that you are alive today, considering the chances of a perfect pregnancy.

My second miscarriage happened at the same point in my pregnancy, nine weeks and three days. This time, however, I almost died in my bathroom. After a very long wait for the doctor to meet with me, following my first ultrasound, I had a bad feeling from the start. I was informed the ultrasound did not indicate any sign of a heartbeat, and the doctor said nothing was growing. I became concerned when I started to bleed and visited my doctor on a Thursday afternoon. She scheduled me for a D&C (dilation and curettage, a surgical procedure often performed after a first-trimester miscarriage) the next Wednesday, the earliest availability to operate. She believed I would be okay until then.

Two days later was a Floyd Mayweather boxing match. I was

entertaining myself doing small chores around the house as a distraction. I put my son to bed, and it was a rather normal, casual Saturday night. Suddenly intense pain struck my lower stomach. I began bleeding out quickly and went to the bathroom. The bleeding became extremely heavy—it felt like an unstoppable raging river. I called the on-call doctor and asked if I should go to the emergency room. She said everything would be okay and to just breathe. "Can you take a deep breath?" the doctor asked over the phone. I was able to do so, so the prognosis was I'd be okay. I did not go to the ER but should have. Less than ten minutes after hanging up the phone, my ears became pressurized and my eyes started to roll. I remember seeing the ceiling and wall mashed up like rubber. I called for my ex-husband (the second) several times and I lost consciousness.

My ex-husband said he luckily caught me as I fell backward. After that, his brother, who was visiting that day, called 911 and an ambulance came quickly. Of course, I don't recall any of it, but I certainly appreciate the timeliness of the first responders.

People sometimes say you see a light when you are close to death, but that was not what I experienced. I luckily gained my awareness slowly, hearing my ex-husband screaming my name, crying, and pleading with me to return to life while I was on the floor still bleeding literally to death. I remember the EMTs, three men and one woman, who took care of me. When I was unconscious, I recall it was like the deepest sleep I have never experienced. It felt like I slept for almost a whole week.

My ex and his brother called our neighbor from Thailand, who was a nursing major, and he came to help me, using his nursing techniques to revive me and his mother's homemade tiger balm as a scent to alert me. I also recall him asking me to hold his finger, but I couldn't. The EMTs placed me on the stretcher and I remember hearing them chatting about the result of the Mayweather boxing match on our way to the elevator. In the ambulance, I received the most painful shot ever on my right hand, which made me scream. I have no idea what it was for, but it was on the back of the right hand and hurt like hell. I remember asking to be taken to Newton-Wellesley Hospital, where my OB-GYN doctor was located. I was told that my blood pressure was too low (sixty on high) and it was dangerous to travel far. Because of this, they took me to the nearest ER.

When I arrived at the hospital, I was basically in the shock stage before a coma. My eyes were bulging open and I had lost more than 50 percent of my blood in a matter of an hour. I learned I was close to having my kidney, liver, heart, and brain shut down from lack of blood within a few hours. I was given a transfusion—three pints of blood in total in twelve hours.

When I informed my mom over an international call about all that transpired, she said, "Wow, you became a US citizen, and now half of your blood will be American, so you are going to be like a half-American now. Make sure to say thank you to your family and your doctor and nurses."

I did try to thank all the doctors and staff. Unfortunately, I could not reach the ambulance staff and EMTs who saved my life, because they left shortly after doing their job and I was too weak at the time to remember to say thank you. But I said, "Thank you! Thank you! Thank you!" to everyone. (Yes, Mom, I said it as you instructed, even when I nearly lost my life.)

I asked one of the nurses how many people it took to contribute one pint of blood. I thought she would say three or four, but she said one, as blood is usually donated in pint increments. I am forever grateful for those random people who donated the blood that courses through me now and send another big thank-you to those anonymous good Samaritans.

Now when I see people waiting to give blood at a local blood drive, I approach them and thank them for saving someone's life, like mine. Because even with our technology-driven society, blood is something we can't generate synthetically yet and is made available only through people's generous donations and their willingness to help random lives.

Just a side story, if I want you to understand my super work ethic, I had two gigs, one on the day I passed out and was in the ER doing the blood transfusion, and one the next day. I asked my ex-husband to call my church job to say I could not make it. The other gig was to play for a local bank's employee appreciation and award ceremony. My close friends came to visit me (thank you, Sandra and Tom) while doing the blood transfusion and I told them I must find a substitute. They knew exactly who to ask and I was able to find a sub for my gig from the hospital. I called the person in charge of the bank and told him about my situation and told him I found a sub so everything would be okay. He sounded shocked and appreciated me arranging that while doing a blood transfusion.

I was discharged the next day, and one of the first phone calls I received on my way home was from the person who subbed for me. His name was Face, and I explained to him as many details as possible and the gig went well. The local bank sent me a bouquet home a few days later, and Face gave me a percentage of his compensation. I was so touched.

Interestingly enough, two of my angels both came and left to heaven at exactly nine weeks and three days—my miscarriages. My birthday is on September 3. Every birthday I get a bit melancholic, thinking if I had not been born on this day, years ago, I wouldn't have had to suffer all the pain I have endured over the years. It has always made my birthday less than a celebratory event for me. But I have gotten beyond it, and part of the reason is truly believing my special angels had a mission: to let me know I was meant to live and to appreciate life no matter what. I believe these special souls are always beside me and are protecting me.

My precious daughter, Jayla Ifunanya Manami Onwuakor, was born on June 1, 2016. *Ifunanya* means "love" in Igbo, a Nigerian Tribe language (my ex-husband is Igbo), and *manami* (愛美) means "beautiful love" in Japanese.

After two miscarriages, I was so nervous I might not be able to conceive or deliver another baby. During my pregnancy with my daughter, everything went wrong. On New Year's Eve 2015, I had a pinched nerve that hurt more than a contraction, and instead of the happy year-end countdown, I was writhing in pain and again was rushed to the ER. I don't believe I've ever cried like a baby from pain in my life. I was concerned about harming the baby, but I took just one painkiller pill at the ER, as the pain was unimaginable. I also suffered with shingles for three weeks during the pregnancy and had a recurrence that lasted about a week. It was so painful, but I endured the pain and suffering without taking medication because I did not want to harm my daughter.

I had a complete placenta previa, which shifted a little, but it led to a C-section. During the C-section, the epidural didn't work after trying for forty-five minutes, and I thought I could not do it anymore due to so much pain from the shots stabbed on my lower spinal cord. Finally, after many failed attempts, the doctors decided to put me under general anesthesia. But in the end, a precious, wonderful baby girl was born. After birth, I struggled with a spinal headache and was told it originated from a small hole made in my spinal cord as part of the epidural procedure. I, therefore, required another procedure called a "blood patch," which involves removing blood out from my arm and injecting it into the spinal cord to seal the hole and prevent spinal fluid leakage, which of course was an extremely painful process. I do not remember the fourth day after my daughter was born due to the spinal headache and the procedure.

For about two weeks I suffered from the aftereffects with excruciating pain from my waist down, and I could not move without screaming. It was an awful and painful experience overall. But when I look at my daughter, so beautiful and precious, healthy and safe, I would not say I forgot the pain, but I know it was worth the real pain.

Looking back, I truly believe my angels in heaven and my daughter taught me to experience extreme physical pain to provide a perspective for living life to its full potential. It certainly has taught me an important lesson: to never take life for granted. When you suffer so much from PTSD and feel the world is closing on you, but there is no physical pain, you get so depressed and feel there is no existence. But after experiencing this magnitude of pain that I had never experienced, I certainly gained a new perspective that pain-free life is wonderful.

APPEARING ON A JAPANESE TV SHOW

During the summer of 2016, I received a call from one of the popular Japanese reality shows, wanting to make a documentary about my life. I answered yes, of course. It was one of my big dreams to be on television and something I've aspired to since I was a little girl. They informed me they had located me via the internet and came to America to film for ten days in October that year. The team comprised of a director, cameraman, and coordinator. The camera crew followed me everywhere for ten days. I carried a tiny microphone inside my clothes.

We journeyed to numerous locations to film, focusing on my

life in America and my ex-husband's Nigerian family. One of the highlights became getting a goat. A lot of Nigerians love eating goat, and every time we go to a zoo or farm, I send goat pictures to my ex-husband and he asks, "How much?" I always have to reply, "They are not for sale." But we did find a farm in Massachusetts where you can purchase a live goat, which they slaughter and prepare for you. The Japanese film crew wanted to film us buying the live goat. In total, they took about eighty hours of film, but much of it was left on the editing floor, as the final product needed to be no more than forty-five minutes. So many scenes were completely cut.

The film wasn't just about my life as a Japanese woman marrying a Nigerian man and living in America, featuring a micro-world (three continents) in one family, but it also consisted of a long interview about my life, and the adversity that comprised so much of it at times. Some of the questions were difficult to answer, such as, "How did you try to kill yourself when you were a teen-ager? What did you use? And what were you thinking?"

I sometimes had to take breaks, go to the bathroom, cry a little and compose myself, and fix my makeup so I didn't look like a panda bear on national TV. Interestingly, one of the questions they asked made me realize something I had never thought about, and therefore had never contemplated an answer to.

I am the type of person who accomplishes many things, good and bad, and sometimes burn myself out. The question they posed to me was, "Why do you thrive so much? What happened in your childhood that influenced you to be such a motivated person?"

I had to stop because I had never considered this until that moment . . . honestly. I do recall one of my counselors conveying there are three main ways many people cope with PTSD: 1) alcohol, 2) drugs, and 3) super achievement. I am allergic to alcohol (I get rashes), so that was never an option for me. I also had asthma, so smoking was not a good option either. Perhaps that left me with option number three. Another possible explanation is that my father used to get angry when I received bad grades. I always ranked among the top five students in my class, sometimes even number one. But because I was running from fear, I honestly don't remember truly learning—it was just that I needed to get there. Gaining an education in fear, under micromanagement, is not the same as learning naturally. There is one incident that occurred when I was in first grade.

In Japan, a parent-teacher conference is an at-home visit. A teacher visits your home and meets with you and your parents. When my first-grade teacher visited my house, she observed to my father that something was wrong. She noted that I seemed to have changed and got quiet. "Is everything okay at home?" she asked.

She was referring, of course, to the time following my mother leaving home. I had tried to pretend everything was normal at school. I smiled; though I interacted well and studied hard during the first grade, I guess I could not trick my teacher. I was shocked my teacher could see something was wrong. I tried so hard to give nothing away, although when you are only seven years old, it's probably not hard for an adult to see. Looking back, I think the shock, confusion, and sadness were there for all to read.

After my teacher's visit, I swore to myself, at age seven, I would do my best to never allow people to see when I am down or sad. I worked as hard as possible to hide my pain and what I was going through via a busy schedule and a thriving lifestyle. So, when asked the question by the TV crew, my brain spun so rapidly and flashed back to that day with my teacher, and it froze me just like I froze during the parent-teacher conference at my home. I told the TV crew that I had never connected the dots between my teacher visiting that day and my achievement. The realization hit me at that moment, and I just started to cry. Of course, with my tears came the panda look, and then I considered that I should not have worn makeup for this interview, especially eyeliner. The things that pass through my head . . .

Despite the intense questions, I enjoyed the filming experience at the many places and activities we shot at. Due to the team's efforts, the show aired across Japan on March 20, 2017. The staff from the TV station emailed me later and told me the official count noted that 7.5 million Japanese people viewed it (as I mentioned earlier)! I can, therefore, say I officially went viral for about an hour.

We expected that many people would want to contact me following the airing of the show, and the TV station asked me if they could give out my email address. I said, of course, I'd be happy to respond to anyone I could help. I received several congratulatory messages from friends, but a few emails from random people reaching out. I did receive a note from a girl who had watched the show, asking if she should continue dating her Nigerian boyfriend. She said she met the Nigerian man in Japan and all her friends were against her dating him because he was a Nigerian and not a typical Japanese. She noted from the show that my ex-husband was Nigerian and sought out my opinion. I told her it doesn't matter where your boyfriend is from. If he treats you with kindness and respect, he's a keeper—it's that simple. I don't know what she decided, but I hope she made her choice on those simple terms and not based on what people said.

Overall, I'd have to say my experience of being on TV was amazing. It truly was a big, big dream come true for me. But the expected paparazzi never showed up after I officially became viral.

BECOMING A JOURNALIST

I grew up in Japan and never spoke a word of English. When I was fourteen years old, my mother found a pen pal program and signed me up for it. I didn't like taking English class in Japan, I thought they were so boring, but since my mom found this pen pal program and found me a lovely pen pal from New Zealand, my interest in speaking English sparked. I so looked forward to receiving a letter from my New Zealander pen pal. We have kept in touch via physical mail (no emails or social media back then), and every time I changed my address, I always told her and she always sent me letters, even when I was in Washington as an exchange student.

Her name is Jolene. We now have social media so we can keep in touch instantly instead of waiting a long time for letters. But if it were not for Jolene, I am not sure where my English-speaking life would be. Thank you, Jolene, for being my lifelong friend and for all our letters that were exchanged to keep me interested in learning English. Unfortunately, I have yet to meet her after all these years of exchanging letters, and I am hoping to meet her in person someday.

Fast-forward to 2020. Very unexpectedly, I became a journalist for *The Foxboro Reporter/The Sun Chronicle* back in October 2017. I have written over two hundred articles so far and taken photos for the stories. I still pinch myself every time my articles get published, especially my many front-cover stories, knowing I have zero education and experience in journalism. I am happy, humbled, and honored to be a reporter and have the opportunity to meet so many inspirational people. When I cover a story, usually people trust me and tell me great stories of their own.

My philosophy in finding good stories are the three Is: Interesting, Inspiring, and Informative. My manager once called me "a story machine," which is one of the biggest compliments for a reporter. I think I just have extreme curiosity and am not afraid to talk to anyone and drill their brains. So here is the crazy story about why and how I became a journalist all of a sudden.

My son, Jaden, sang the National Anthem at Boston City Hall Plaza in August 2017 for the Boston GreenFest (thanks to Karen). I accompanied on piano for him and our story was in *The Boston Globe* (thank you, Paul, for writing our story) and *The Foxboro Reporter*. You can come to my website, jurilove.com, and click on "Press" to find the articles.

Rick was the one who wrote the front-cover article for *The Foxboro Reporter*, and he is an amazing person I was fortunate to have met. He came to a Foxboro Rotary meeting to cover stories and saw I was connected to a lot of things (I am a Rotarian at Foxboro Rotary Club). Rick asked me, "Juri, you seem to be connected to many things. If you find any potential stories, can you let me know?" The next day, I gave him five leads, and two got published right away.

He saw some potential in me and asked me to meet his manager at *The Sun Chronicle*. When I met the manager, Craig, I had zero expectation that I would ever become a journalist. All I talked to the manager was about *Spotlight*, the movie featuring four *Boston Globe* reporters. One of the reporters happened to be his close and longtime friends, so we talked a lot about how journalism can bring justice to many social issues, and how otherwise it would not have a voice. Surprisingly, I got the job, and ever since then I have been publishing many articles, which is unbelievable knowing my English grades were not great when I was in school in Japan.

I am so grateful to be a journalist. I think the most fun part is meeting many people from different backgrounds and professions, and I am constantly learning something new every day. It is also empowering to see your story get published in the newspaper and then see the paper everywhere in stores as well as online. As I explained earlier, a tangible, measurable outcome is one of the keys to self-confidence and to building strong resilience. Therefore, every week I feel my confidence boosting, and the publication is contributing to my resilience to heal and overcome my PTSD in a wider perspective.

I am so grateful for the new opportunity and being able to use my press pass to talk to anyone. In each article I would interview many people. To be honest, sometimes I would forget people's names, and I still feel horrible when people say, "Hi, Juri" and I am like, "Hi . . ." In my mind, I am saying, *OMG, I have to go back to the article I wrote and figure out what the person's name was.*

It has truly been a life-changing opportunity to be able to empower myself and others, advocate others' voices, and publish it. And especially with online versions, you never know who you are reaching out to. It is so amazing to hear from random people about how much they enjoyed my articles. I thank my lifelong pen pal, Jolene. And I also thank my mother for finding a program at the local post office three decades ago. All of my past articles can be read on muckrack.com/jurilove. I would like to sincerely thank Rick, Craig, Jeff, and Sue at *The Sun Chronicle* for giving me this opportunity to be a reporter.

I also would like to note I started to volunteer at Foxboro Cable Access, where I am grateful to be working with a wonderful team. I volunteer as an assistant producer for a talk show called *Around Foxboro*. Sometimes I host the TV show as well. I also started and produced a Foxboro Youth Production show called *What's Up!*. Both programs can be seen at fcatv.org. Thank you, Michael, Paul,

Lauren, and Margaret for trusting me and giving me these opportunities as well. Foxboro Cable Access generously gave me two awards—Rookie of the Year 2018 and Volunteer of the Year 2019—which I am truly humbled and grateful for. You can now see my name on a plaque when you enter the building.

ABOUT FORGIVENESS

People have told me at various points in my life that I should forgive and let go of my trauma. I was never able to forgive and forget, and I doubt I will ever be able to do so. I know people have good intentions and speak to me out of concern about my situation, wanting only the best for me. However, after much consideration about forgiveness, I have concluded that there are certain things you are *never* allowed to forgive and be okay with. What I have come to terms with is being able to forgive myself for not forgiving perpetrators. This concept helped me tremendously, and I hope this will help someone reading my book. I know many people may disagree, but many people may think this concept makes the most sense.

In my case, I do not want to forgive my father. Because of him, I have lived several years in hell and will never know what a healthy father-daughter relationship is. Nor will I ever be able to place my faith in humanity, and despite all my searching, because of the trauma he inflicted, I may never feel at peace. If you are also a survivor of abuse in any form, please don't feel pressured to forgive your perpetrator. And do not feel pressure from the people who keep telling you to let go and forgive so it will all be better. If you find peace in doing so, then more power to you, but know there is solace in forgiving yourself for not forgiving. This is just my solution and how I stay sane through each day.

Forgive yourself for not forgiving someone who hurt you. In my opinion, that is completely healthy and wise.

A lot of times, I get angry when people who have fortunately never experienced the degree of trauma I experienced may casually say, "Oh, just forget about it, you will be fine, just forgive and move on, you are thinking too deeply, you are crazy, you are depressed and negative, etc." When it comes to forgiveness, many people think it is the best way to cope with the trauma. But let me tell you something—at least in my case, there will be no justice made for the rest of my life. Who can ever forgive a child sex abuser who has never been charged for the sin he committed? Let me be the one who knows the truth of simply right or wrong, and let me SPEAK OUT that I HAVE A CHOICE to forgive myself for never forgiving perpetrators. But again, I have *no* desire to bring him to justice, because that will never change anything that happened to me nor the pain it caused. I am fine with it. I developed my defense mechanism and came to peace with the unique concept I developed over the years.

ABOUT HAPPINESS

Over the years, I have come to learn a few things about happiness. The reason you are "unhappy" is entirely the concept you have in your head. You have determined that your situation is not satisfactory and have made yourself unhappy. If you want to "feel happy," experience happiness; it is a simple trigger that you stimulate by your train of thoughts. The main ingredients of happiness are optimism and positivity. Even if millions of people admire your life because what they see seems so happy, if you are not feeling that happiness, it is all pointless. Many people wish to be happy, but the truth is happiness is right in front of you; you just need to affirm it. To become happy, you must learn the method of how to feel happiness. One of my close friends suggested inhaling deeply while saying, "I love my life," then exhaling, chanting, "I appreciate my life." Repeat this for some time . . .

Take it from me. Even if you have endured much hardship and adversity, you can train your brain to look for happiness and find what happiness is.

Personally, seeing the smiles of my children makes me happy, and that is a perfect example of the triumph and affirmation of overcoming my trauma. Accepting the compliments from others, not crying every day, being able to see the world positively, not taking every action from others as something against you, and building strength around whatever you can hold on to—every day you live, breathe, have a good night's sleep, and wake up again is a victory. It sounds small, but it was so difficult before because I was an extremely unhappy person. Sometimes it is hard to keep being happy, but all I can say is it is in your brain, and *you* have 100 percent control over feeling happiness. It is within you.

CHAPTER 7

My Message

TO THE VICTIM

When no one is there for you, and no one believes you or your story, remember one thing: You did nothing wrong! Nothing! People will tell you, oh, just forget about it. Forgive! Move on. But I can truly tell you from my experience, it is not that simple and clean. The first step is to realize and admit you are the victim. People may tell you, "Stop victimizing yourself," but that is not good advice—some incidents are simply wrong. Things happen quickly without your control, and to be honest, amidst it all, there is not much you can do unless you recognize what's happening. There is a technique I learned that I could share, but when you are in the middle of the storm, things go downhill faster than you could ever imagine.

The first thing you need to know is that people are willing to help. It can be difficult reaching out and trusting people with such sensitive information, but in truth, most people, if asked, are empathetic and willing to help.

You can't get help if you don't ask. "I need help!" And if the person does not believe your story, do not give up, and ask another person until you can really get help. Do not give up on finding the right person or agency who can help your case. Remember the law of averages.

Far too many people who are victims and who falsely blame themselves for their situation feel they cannot reach out. Fear is another reason some people feel boxed in by their situation and don't ask for help. Sadly, a lot of perpetrators can brainwash you deeply that you are the wrong one, and they did you a favor. But please, please do not be manipulated by this. Never listen to them, and instead listen to your instinct that you did nothing wrong. WRONG IS WRONG. I've heard of some cases where the perpetrator will threaten to harm the victim's loved ones if they tell their secret (the abuse), so the victim becomes too scared to tell anyone. But I wish for you to see that as a complete brainwash. It makes me so angry that people, especially children, are threatened, because not only do they get violated, but their voices, too, are taken away.

Please trust me when I say speaking up and uttering the words, "I need help," changes everything. If you can't bring yourself to ask it of others because you feel trapped, simply say it to yourself. "I am not okay, I need help!" For the longest time, I could not say that, so I understand your pain.

If you're in a bad situation, it may take more than asking for help. You may need the courage to physically separate yourself from the issue. That was what I did back when I was thirteen years old. I told myself, "I need to escape from this hell," and I did, courageously.

It is not an easy thing to do, but I promise you it will not last forever. You owe yourself the opportunity to change from victim to survivor. You have a right to live a happy and fulfilling life.

Here are some things to keep in mind at those times when you feel life is against you:

- It is NOT your fault. It is NOT your fault.

- Remember, you came to this earth with lots of hopes and aspirations.
- Please know your life is precious. Your life is meaningful, and your life can continue.
- I have so much love and compassion for you.
- I understand you and I cry with you, not for you.
- Your tears are mine. It is something that needs to be shed out for you to evolve.
- Don't ever think you need to overcome this. No, there is no pressure, no deadline, no right or wrong about who you are.
- You are dealing with so much that not many people can comprehend.
- You have an absolute right to vent, cry, collapse, and stop what you are doing.
- Stand in front of the mirror and say, "I am beautiful. No one can take my spirit away from me. I deserve to be happy."

To the victim, I care for you and I believe in you, even if no one else does. Your perpetrator may create a perfect manipulation scheme from which he/she believes you'll never survive. But do not worry. Justice will prevail in the end in many forms. There is one person who knows you are right—that person is *you*. So why care if no one understands you?

Some people out there are truly genuine and willing to help. If you meet someone like that, don't ever take advantage of their kindness. Don't ever think they will fix you. They offer to lend you their knowledge, time, compassion, and resources, but they have their own families to care for and lives to live. So, appreciate their help, but know at the end of the day, *you need to stand up for yourself*. It might be scary, but you can do it. Sometimes you have to realize you just need to hustle it out, power through, and conquer the adversity. Know that I am right here with you on this journey.

Go to a local police station, call support-based agencies, reach out to friends, text, email, social media, whatever it takes to get the help you need. Be smarter than the perpetrator and manipulate them back hard to survive.

Be smart, always be careful, and stay alive.

Your best friend is your instinct.

You are born to live, not to die.

It took some time for me to realize and accept how unfair it is that justice may not always prevail. Yet justice resides not only in the court of law but also within your heart. In the court of *your heart*, know you are justified!

Also, one important thing. If the perpetrators are your parents, uncle, aunt, siblings, or some older family members, you owe them NO RESPECT. Respect is something that must be earned in any role. Even if you are the CEO of a company, if you commit a crime, you are a criminal. It's as simple as that. Because you are a parent or older role model does not mean you are perfect.

Especially in my case, I struggled so much with this concept since in Japan there is so much ethical and moral pressure that as a child you must obey your parents or older/respectable figures and respect them no matter what. But there is no obligation to respect assholes, criminals, or people who hurt you. Some people pressure you saying, "Blood is thicker than water," but I think the concept is questionable. I think respect is something that should never be automatically given.

I think parenting has no prerequisite besides having sex and getting pregnant. But there should be more than that. For some professions, you must study, go to college, pass a board exam to be a doctor, etc. But not for becoming a parent. There is no regulation to be one, and though I think in some cases there should be, that's not the reality. Therefore, from a child's perspective, you owe *no* respect if your parent hurt you, and I hope you are able to get help from professionals. I think in America there are many social services and other interventions available.

Japan is changing its perception of sexual abuse from parents, teachers, and other respectable figures, but I don't think it is up to the level of American agencies who can protect children. However, I've heard more victims in Japan have started to speak out about sexual abuse, which they have the complete right to, and of course, the #MeToo movement has been helping. It is extremely important that everyone knows their rights.

I recently watched *Jeffrey Epstein: Filthy Rich* on Netflix. After watching way too many victims speak out about their experiences, I froze for several hours because their facial expressions and stories reminded me of my exact past. So many flashbacks played in my mind, even some memories I had completely forgotten. What all the victims explained was, sadly, the same as what I felt. They froze when it happened and they didn't know what to say, and some said they could not tell anyone what happened.

It is devastating to see these repeated sex offender stories, but as one of the victims of sex abuse, I am hoping that by telling our survival stories, victims will eventually make more notions and movement to pressure the perpetrators and people around us who can stand with us. I deeply appreciate the producer of this show, who told the truth about the Epstein case, just like the movie *Spotlight*, which I was extremely empowered by.

In a perfect world, there should not be child sex abuse, but unfortunately, we hear way too many stories. If you can think of any solution with me and act on it in our lifetime, please be the change you want to see to protect one more victim. And to the victims, I believe we have the power to prevent future crimes with courage, wisdom, and instinct. And that is part of my motivation and one of the reasons why I am compelled to tell my story unapologetically.

RAINN (Rape, Abuse & Incest National Network) is the nation's largest anti–sexual violence organization that you can reach out to (rainn.org, 1-800-656-HOPE (4673)).

TO THE PERPETRATOR

If you are a perpetrator, chances are you are not reading this book. If there is a slight chance my message can reach you, I hope you will consider my words very carefully.

There are those people who believe your upbringing, family, and perhaps the experience of being abused yourself have a huge role in your behavior. That would mean, then, that I, too, could become a perpetrator because my upbringing checks all these boxes. But I am not. You have made a choice—a conscious choice.

Have you considered why you were born? What your true purpose in life is? Do you truly believe you are born on this earth to hurt and ruin another person's life? Is it to justify the wrongs that have been done to you?

Think again about why you were born. Some theories might argue you were born to harm so that the world may know the comparison of bad to good. So the victim might learn about life and grow from the experience. But as a victim myself, let me set you straight—that is complete rubbish. The truth is right or wrong, and wrong is wrong. My nine-year-old son understands this concept, and even most kindergarteners know this. Why has it gotten so complicated to where it must involve so many agencies, police, lawyers, and the court system? When you do something wrong, you admit it and express your sincere apology. How simple is that?

You may not be forgiven, but that is not the point. You did something wrong. You apologize and never do it again. For many twisted, distorted souls who are lost and somehow believe they have a mission to be bad, do you have any idea of the consequences you leave behind? The physical and mental effects of your actions will haunt your victims for almost the rest of their lives. Some may not even be able to survive. Even those who do will live with the pain and trauma for a very long time. The victims may end up being addicted to drugs or alcohol, or even commit suicide because of the action that was done to them. The truth is, there is no excuse for what you have done or what you are doing. Justice will prevail, and if not, karma usually finds a way to intervene and even it up.

Despite your anger, your feelings of not being heard, or maybe being a victim yourself, there is no excuse for exacting your frustration on another person. I have zero compassion for you because you have chosen to hurt someone, rather than seek out other means of help. Even those you hurt could be someone who could help you. Such an act is unacceptable. If you are willing to change, do so today. Change is scary for all of us, but please know it can be done. You may not realize it, but let me look dead in your soul and eyes. I see your fear, I know your feelings of inferiority. I can look into your eyes again and again and say there is no excuse not to change, to avoid hurting precious lives at all cost. If no one has ever told you to apologize for your actions and own your mistakes, I am telling you now to admit and apologize. Do not waste your precious life on this earth. You could be helping someone instead of hurting someone. So please change for yourself and so you can preclude any further episodes of anyone getting hurt by you. If you don't know what to do, seek a counselor or other professional means of help.

Did you know research shows each perpetrator affects an average of six victims? So if you can stop, there won't be more victims. Change is scary, but please consider helping yourself and helping others. I don't want to see any more children crying, any more victims, or any more violence. Let's just focus on creating something positive, because your life *will* end someday, and that might be today.

TO THE FAMILY AND
FRIENDS AROUND THE VICTIM

You have the most important key to opening a slim door that is about to close forever. That slim chance is when the victim opens their mouth to tell you the most traumatic story they have sadly experienced. You might be the last person on this earth the victim, who can be a child or an adult, can talk to.

My wish is that you will never say, "You made that up," "That's not believable," "I don't have time for it," or "You are kidding." These statements are poison. The victim's trust in humanity has already been destroyed from being violated. Not only in my case but from listening to other cases and writing many stories as a journalist, many do not believe sexual assault stories or give appropriate support.

Why?

If I had to make a wild guess, it is from the basic fear that people do not believe others could do such a thing. But the reality is it unfortunately happens. As a Rotarian, I worked to host the Human Trafficking Summit in Foxboro, Massachusetts, and through the process, I also learned of many victims who were denied by society. If you are someone who has had a chance to hear a victim's story, please do not ever doubt them. Please listen to them and take appropriate action. Think about it—why the hell would someone make up a story to get your attention when they are really hurt? It is not about getting any attention; it is crying out loud for help. After the victim gets violated, they gained the courage to share with someone they thought they could trust, which is one of the hardest things to do. I know this from my own experience.

So please do not ever doubt them, but instead learn about their experience, gain knowledge of what sexual abuse is, and reach out to the agency and be an advocate, especially for children who cannot advocate well for themselves. My counselor once told me 80 percent of mothers do not believe their partner has sexually abused their child. According to this statistic, my mother fits that majority, but I wish she had been one of the 20 percent who could have believed my story. But I believe that education and awareness can lower that 80 percent to zero someday, and I know we have a long road ahead of us in order to do so. Educating yourself on the reality of sexual abuse is crucial to prevent the second or third wave of shock after the initial incidents. I have done many motivational speeches and shared my own stories, and you have no idea how many people have come to me and told me of their own sad sexual abuse story, which they said they have never told to anyone but me. I am humbled to hear they can trust me that much, but why can't society embrace and believe that these things happen way too often? That way we can be better prepared to be a safety net if, unfortunately, sexual abuse happens.

Darkness to Light provides great awareness training in our community. I have taken their online course, and it was empowering and useful. I highly recommend taking this training by visiting their website, d2l.org.

A Lesson from Lions

AT THE PROLOGUE, I WROTE ABOUT TWO BROKEN SOULS. One soul, whom I met in Israel, taught me a lesson about lions. When lions hunt animals, the oldest male roams the savanna while the others hide in the bushes. When the prey sees the male lion, they seek refuge, running toward the bushes, where the other lions wait. The lesson here is that when you are afraid, you tend to run away. But often, running from a problem only leads to bigger problems.

For many of the adversities I have experienced, I ran away, never facing them fully, thinking they would fade away. But instead, they haunted me, eating me up physically and mentally for most of my life. I regret not facing them sooner. Now, I know I need to believe I am wise and strong enough to run toward the fear and face the truth, and never run away from it. I know I can do it, and so can you. When you are afraid, realize that fear originates in your brain. You create the fear and allow it to become a monster, sometimes so real you become trapped within. Not so many people understand, but I think the truth is fear is made out of love.

Love can be a joy. But because of love, people hurt themselves and others, which can destroy so many things. In my case, the pure concept of wanting to be loved and giving pure love back to someone who should be protecting me was shattered by my horrific childhood. Then fear took over and I wanted to be loved and give love, but it never seemed possible. During my adulthood, this affected me deeply and I was always confused about how to love because of the distorted way I was shown.

No one could explain to me why I lived in fear. It was almost a lifelong, winding road that seems to go back to my father and what he has done to me. For the longest time, I believed I would never gain nor experience the concept of pure love for the rest of my life. But I do believe I can give pure love to someone who deserves it, especially to myself. I need wisdom and courage to sharpen it, and I need to trust that I have a burning innocence that was never violated by anyone and that I can share with the world.

When my son, Jaden, and daughter, Jayla, came to my life, this fear started to fade away. The love they have shown me has been so pure. The idea of wanting to be loved and to give love became real without any consequences. My fear was replaced with their unconditional love toward me and my infinite love toward them. If I had never faced the truth regarding fear and had kept running away from it, I would have never felt true happiness and love from others, especially from my angels, Jaden Chidubem Isamu (勇) Onwuakor and Jayla Ifunanya Manami (愛美) Onwuakor. I love you both so much from bottom of my heart. Thank you for helping Mommy learn not to run away from fear and to be simply be able to love and be loved.

MY GRATITUDE

My two angels, my true gifts, my gifted and handsome son, Jaden, and my precious princess, Jayla . . . I love you so very much. I know you both will make a positive impact on many lives, just as you already have on your mother. Thank you for coming into my life and teaching me how to love myself. Thanks also to my family in Japan, and to the many close friends whom I now call my extended American family.

Ed Little, my mentor who is watching over me from heaven—without you believing in me, back from when I was eighteen years old until you passed, I would not be here sharing my music and living happily. Thank you, Ed. I love you!

To my many true and close friends who have encouraged me to *live* and continue my journey when I did not want to, thank you for your support and true love. You helped me restore the faith I lost when I was a little girl.

People come and go. But to all the people I have met since I was born, I appreciate all the lessons I have learned from you.

To the people I love and people who generously love me, thank you.

To Master Christopher Rappold from Personal Best Karate for motivating me to finish my book.

To the amazing author Ken Paiva, who has spent many hours editing my first-ever book and doing a masterful job. And to his friend Smita Bhat and my wonderful friend Dr. Geraldine Bloustien, who proofread and edited this book for me. Yosef Yisrael and the team at BookLogix, thank you for coming into my life to help me publish this book.

I thank you, the reader, for finding my book and taking time out of your busy schedule to read the story of my life.

For those who are going through adversity and any traumatic event right now, please know it will pass. Nothing stays the same. Recognize that you have total control of your situation and can choose to be a victim or be a survivor. My advice for you is to be a survivor. I have unconditional love for you and faith that you will overcome your adversity just like I did. Please count on me on this.

Continue to live even when the trauma acts up and feels like it can destroy your life. Please remember love is the cause of your fears, tears, and any hate you harbor. You just must know that.

It is okay to love yourself, and I know everything will be ok.

Thank you very much for reading my book until the end. It means a lot to me that you made it all the way here to learn about my life. Thank you.

I can be reached by email at juripanda@gmail.com.

I am open to any suggestions or discussions, and I will be happy to come to speak at an event to share my life story with your peers.

Life is something you create and that you are responsible for.

If there is no road, or if there seems to be no way, know you have the power to create, pave, and walk the road you desire. Remember, it is all in your head, and you have the power to conquer this mystery called life and love.

By now, I must say another gift I gained from my adversity is perspective. I have gained a perspective that protects me from breaking down to pieces, and that perspective is the power and knowledge you can learn from being open-minded and willing to heal.

With my eternal love and gratitude,
Juri Love

ABOUT THE AUTHOR

Juri Love was born on September 3, 1976, in Japan. Juri came to America when she was seventeen as a part of the Japanese government–supported youth program, and she was greeted by the Crown Prince and Crown Princess at the time, now the Emperor and Empress of Japan, at the Tokyo Imperial Palace before her departure.

Juri is a scholarship recipient of Berklee College of Music. She has toured nationally, and has performed, recorded, and produced many albums. She is a former founder/president of Genuine Voices, a nonprofit that taught music in juvenile detention centers. Juri is also a recipient of the "Heroes Among Us" Award from the NBA Boston Celtics, the Volunteerism Award from the New England Patriots, and the Paul Harris Fellow Award from Rotary International. Her inspiring life has been featured in many media, including a Japanese reality show that aired in 2017 and was viewed by 7.5 million people.

She has spoken as a guest speaker at Berklee College of Music; Wheelock College; Showa University; Career TEAM; Nagareyama City in Chiba, Japan; Plugged-In Teen Band Program; the Women United for the Advancement of African Countries Conference; Newton, Braintree, Mansfield, and Needham Rotary Clubs in

Massachusetts; Arizona State University; IASPM (International Association for the Study of Popular Music) in Rome; Northeastern University; the DECA Conference; and many more.

Also known as the "Goddess of Connection," Juri is a musician, journalist, model, actor, survivor of sexual abuse, physical abuse, and homelessness, motivational speaker, TV show and podcast host, TV show and film producer, Reiki practitioner, life coach, and Rotarian.

Juri is a single mother of two (Jaden and Jayla) who enjoys and cherishes her life and motherhood fully.

Visit her website at jurilove.com.

CPSIA information can be obtained
at www.ICGtesting.com
Printed in the USA
LVHW040344301020
670143LV00010B/102